HACK YOUR MOTIVATION™

ALSO BY THE AUTHOR

Motivation for Learning and Performance

Dr. Bobby Hoffman

HACK
YOUR
MOTIVATION

OVER **50** SCIENCE-BASED STRATEGIES
TO IMPROVE PERFORMANCE

A⋅P ATTRIBUTION PRESS • OVIEDO FL

Hack Your Motivation
Over 50 Science-Based Strategies to Improve Performance

by Dr. Bobby Hoffman

Published by
Attribution Press
P.O. Box 623342
Oviedo, Florida 32762

ISBN: 978-0-9988457-2-2 trade paperback
        978-0-9988457-3-9 electronic book

Visit www.hackyourmotivation.com

Contact the author at hackyourmotivation@gmail.com

First printing

Design and composition: www.dmargulis.com
Cover design: Hannah Carter

Manufactured in the United State of America

This book is dedicated to my late son, Robert, who taught me that understanding our motives is indeed a slippery slope. Finding your path intentionally is far better than discovering it by chance.

CONTENTS

Contents

MOTIVATION HACK

The knowledge, strategies, and skills needed to effectively and efficiently improve your life, reach your desired goals, and achieve personal success

AUTHOR'S NOTE: To view lively video discussions of selected book passages and many of the Hacks, download a QR reader to your smart phone. Then scan the QR codes found throughout the book to instantly watch the videos.

Feel free to share the videos with your friends and colleagues!

Preface

Mischievous behavior

HACK YOUR MOTIVATION IS the book I wasn't allowed to write last time. My former editor warned me that writing this book would forever label me a "narcissist," because I planned to tell candid stories about real people and use intimate examples of my own twisted behavior and motives to make practical, scientifically based points about motivation. This is the book that was labeled too raw, brash, and frank to be printed by traditional publishers—you know, the type that operate under antiquated business models, have inflexible corporate policies, and allow editorial censorship. No surprise there: the unconventional is often met with resistance. My last book, published in 2015 by one of the largest academic publishers in the world, earned the **#1 new book rank** in Cognitive Psychology on Amazon.com. You can buy that book for around seventy dollars—please do!—or you can read this book, the one I really wanted to write. Shrewd people will welcome this book with an open mind because it offers concise, easy-to-implement, and scientifically supported motivational knowledge and strategies that most of us need for success.

First this happens

This book is not designed to make you feel warm and fuzzy right away; it is designed to teach you the skills and strategies that can make you happier in the long run. After you read this book, you may not spring out of bed like a hyperactive kangaroo, but you will know why sometimes you want to hide under the covers. Unlike other authors, I don't promise that once you master the book's content you will be richer or smarter. I do promise that you will know research-supported strategies from psychology, business, education, athletics, and neuroscience that can propel you to personal success and professional accomplishment. Many of us expect instant results from motivational advice because late-night infomercials and pretend academics make shallow promises based on unsupported claims. These promises are designed to make you feel good, create dependence on the sellers, and separate you from your money. **Before you read one more word,** remember: no book and no other person can make you excel. You know better than anyone else what contributes to your feelings of satisfaction and well-being. But you probably *don't* know the scientifically based strategies—the maneuvers I call **Hacks**—that, once mastered, will accelerate your motivational growth.

Here's the difference
Like many people, you probably lie in bed some mornings trying to motivate yourself to get up and get going. Maybe you hit snooze over and over; maybe you search for reasons to endure the grind of physical or emotional discomfort, exerting strenuous effort, or tolerating annoying people. Other days, you rise renewed and invigorated, confident that nothing could possibly interfere with a satisfying and productive day. On those days, you feel strong, capable, and competent, knowing you will reach goals that will benefit you and others. The difference between people who (literally or figuratively) go back to sleep and people who seem to have supernatural motivation is the realization that life is full of opportunities to be reached and obstacles meant to be overcome. However, without knowledge of the Hacks in this book, your potential is restricted, your effort can stall, and your accomplishments and satisfaction will be limited.

This is what happens next
The science of motivation is abundantly clear about what happens when you use the Hacks described in this book. The payoff is immense. Appropriate strategy use leads to achievement, achievement creates elevated mood and positive emotion, and people with

positive emotions rate their lives more favorably, reporting consistently stronger feelings of happiness, relaxation, and contentment. And the Hacks don't just make you feel better. Although we should be careful when inferring that one thing caused another, positive emotions bring with them distinct health and financial benefits. General feelings of well-being and psychological satisfaction are linked to stronger resistance to common cold viruses, quicker recovery from illnesses (including cancer), and longer lives. When you feel better, your energy will increase; you will sleep better, eat better, and have more (and better) sex. People who have stronger feelings of well-being are perceived as more social, demonstrate more creativity, and tend to be well liked. Happy people more frequently donate their time to help those in need and are more likely to be optimistic about the future. People who feel good score more job interviews, have higher performance ratings at work, and earn more money. But *first you must master the Hacks.*

YouTube video: Why Read This Book?

Why some people will shun this book

I work with brilliant people, but my esteemed colleagues—leaders in the fields of psychology and education—may snub this book. *Hack Your Motivation* doesn't fit the tedious, jargon-filled style of most evidence-based writing, which is churned out by cookie-cutter academics who must publish their work (for free!) in scientific, peer-reviewed journals. I should know—I'm tenured faculty at one of the largest research universities in the world and have published plenty of conventional journal articles to meet the expectations set forth in my job description. You can read some of my articles on Google Scholar, if you are so inclined. (Not many people read journal articles—mostly begrudging students whose instructors require them to and academics who need the information to advance their own research agendas and careers. I don't blame you if you don't.)

This book will also annoy the imposters—the self-proclaimed business and industry consulting "experts" with little background knowledge about the topics that they publish on and profit from. I know what that industry is like too: I spent twenty years working as a leadership and performance consultant before changing careers, sacrificing a lucrative business to earn my PhD. I call these authors "karaoke academics"—they generalize findings they skim from journal articles, provide shallow, misleading interpretations of the research, and ultimately misrepresent the original author's intention to make a buck. These imposters simply repackage and sell the ideas of my brilliant colleagues who publish their research in academic journals to earn tenure. When it comes to music, wouldn't you prefer to listen to the original artist's version rather than a bad karaoke imitation? Shouldn't the same rules apply to knowledge about the latest findings and strategies from motivational science? Given the choice, I think you will agree that the original source is better.

Hack Your Motivation gives you the most accurate and up-to-date information on motivation to help improve your life. This book is written in an **informal** and **amusing** style. The unorthodox examples from my life are meant to enlighten, inspire, and entertain. The strategies and tips you will find in this book are all based on hardcore motivational science, but it isn't theory-laden gobbledygook—you know, the kind where you read the same sentences two or three times and *still* can't figure out what the author is talking about or why you should care.

If you want to make your life easier, if feeling positive about yourself is important to you, and if you want to master strategies for success while gaining a better understanding of who you are and why you do what you do, then please continue reading *Hack Your Motivation,* and share what you learn with others. If you prefer to take your motivational science in a 435-page technical version with hundreds of citations, then please feel free to buy my other book! Both books are based on the latest objective research and are designed to improve your life. Only you know which approach works best for you, no matter what those other motivational imposters tell you. *Now, let's get hacking!*

A special note for researchers, scientists, PhDs, and academics

This book is based entirely on science, but if you want dense empirical study descriptions, methodological critiques, and evidence-based documentation of inferences, look elsewhere. The entire point of this book is to transform the current scientific evidence about motivation into practice, a goal many academics often discuss but rarely reach. If you would like a citation or documentation for anything in this book, or if you wish to tell me what you think, please reach out to me directly via email at hackyourmotivation@gmail.com and I will be more than happy to respond. I look forward to hearing from you!

Bobby Hoffman

April 4, 2017

CHAPTER ONE

Game Changers

GWB, the majestic gateway to adolescent adventure

The playing fields

SPEEDING ACROSS THE GEORGE Washington Bridge at eighty miles an hour toward New York City and cruising down the dilapidated West Side Highway to score a five-dollar bag of weed didn't seem like such a bad idea in 1973. It seemed harmless to pile five stoned guys into my '62 Bel Air, although we were stopped by the cops at least once a week just for looking sketchy. Driving to the city was almost a daily ritual back then. We all chipped in a dollar in exchange for a few puffs and the predictable Colombian nirvana, courtesy of our acquaintance Orlando. We were occasionally ripped off (once with a machete to the throat), but things usually worked out flawlessly. Well, at least up until the time Dwayne got a ticket for reckless driving, speeding, and toll evasion when he was at the helm of our cannabis caravan. The price of paying the fines would have bought fifty nickel bags, and, as I recall, we did not chip in to pay it. The stunt cost Dwayne about two hundred and fifty bucks, but he solidified his reputation as the Road King of Fort Lee, New Jersey, for many years to come.

Weekends were even more exciting. We focused on gambling, sex, or some combination of the two. The Riverview gang, or, as we referred to ourselves, the Fearsome Fivesome, were armed with savings-bank envelopes full of minimum-wage cash from our various jobs. On weekends, we made some extra stops on the regular run to New York City, and where we stopped depended on who had the most convincing argument that day—and where we were in the teenage hormonal cycle (p. 65). In '73, New York City mayor John Lindsay was not interested in cleaning up the city's shady side. We either blew our weekly paychecks at the racetrack, betting on trotters, or (after scoring weed) we made an extra stop at The Meeting Room, where young ladies were willing to provide sexual favors for the very reasonable price of ten dollars. I never participated in those carnal pleasures. I alternated between standing guard in the dank, smelly stairway, waiting for the boys to return from their ten-minute adventure, and waiting outside to be sure my double-parked car wasn't being stolen by local entrepreneurs or towed by the mayor's vigilant parking posse.

YouTube video:
Game Changers

My decision to forego these pay-for-pleasure escapades humiliated me for years; I was teased by my buddies for my questionable libido (p. 85). This was the first time I noticed that, despite the stout kinship among my friends, our motives, priorities, and behaviors were sometimes radically different (p. 90). The divide didn't bother me that much—I had different gratification beliefs than my friends, but I knew that we also had plenty in common. We were a clique. We were not nerds, heads, jocks, or greasers (the usual categories [p. 55] back then). We were just a tight-knit bunch of guys with shared likes and needs (mostly playing cards, drinking beer, and searching for lonely girls) who admired and approved of certain behaviors and dismissed outsiders. We had no qualms about denying people admission to our personal fraternity if they didn't meet our arbitrary, never-discussed qualifications.

There were many moments of adolescent absurdity. Once, on a munchie run, my friend Scott parked in front of the 7-Eleven where

I worked for years. We were inside the store when I saw someone accidentally back their car into Scott's front bumper. His car began rolling backward across a major intersection, cars crazily honking at the driverless vehicle, which hit a No Parking sign. It halted momentarily, then the gas tank exploded, leaking gas all over the church parking lot where the car eventually died. The Fearsome Fivesome had inadvertently created a glorious opportunity for the valiant fire department of Fort Lee, New Jersey, to spring into action and display their skills. Less than five minutes later, the intersection was closed, sirens were wailing, and my friends Scott and Flip were spread-eagled against a fire truck being searched. The overzealous firefighters had concluded that Scott was in the car, recklessly driving backward, not in the 7-Eleven deciding between Twinkies and a bottle of Yoo-Hoo. The fire chief detained them both until the police arrived. My friends were the probably the first idiots ever busted by a volunteer fire department. Meanwhile, I ran away at full speed.

You'll find many more tales of tomfoolery, shenanigans, and malarkey throughout this book, but you're probably wondering what these stories have to do with motivation or motivational Hacks. The

Two-fifths of the Riverview gang

answer is, *plenty*! These stories are examples of motivated action, illustrated through the commonplace behaviors of my friends, my family, and myself. Exploring and interpreting these behaviors will help you understand the underlying motives that produced them while building your knowledge of motivational science. Every single important event and person in our lives can potentially influence the development of motives. Our motives drive behaviors, and our behaviors show the world how we believe life should be led.

I refer to these influential life events and people as **game changers**. Our reactions to the people, places, challenges, rewards, and failures in our lives ultimately reveal what motivates us and why. Not every incident is a game changer, of course—each person values daily encounters differently than others, and sometimes differently from our previous selves. What seems critical on Monday may be an afterthought by Friday. Were any of the events described above game changers for me? Probably not, but the stories hold important clues to self-awareness and understanding. These clues help us accurately assess motives so we can choose and implement the right Hacks.

If you are looking for an easy way to discover your motives and assess game changers in your own life, you will probably be frustrated with this book. Despite what the other motivation "experts" would like you to believe, there are no instant solutions. Understanding our motives and beliefs requires examining patterns over time, not looking at a single, isolated instance of behavior or labeling ourselves based on a brief survey. Reaching accurate conclusions about ourselves is further complicated: the same behavior may be caused by several different motives (p. 68), and you are probably the worst judge of your own motives. Many of our self-assessments are flawed because we selectively pay attention to what we believe is important, change our behavior based on who we are with, and view the world through a lens shaped by our culture. In addition, many motives operate below the level of consciousness. Deducing motives from behavior requires deep reflection and accurate interpretation to determine who you are, who you want to be, and why you do what you do.

You will eventually identify your own game changers and motives, even the hidden ones. Two major themes of this book are self-discovery and personal awareness. But first you will chuckle, groan, and gasp reading about more of my chicanery. Through my narrative of a sixty-year ride on the roller coaster of life that included giving up a lucrative career, working at more than fifty companies and four universities, marrying the wrong woman, getting fired, being plowed down by a speeding car, burying a child, and writing books, you will learn how to accurately analyze your own life and decipher which people, places, things, beliefs, and opportunities influenced you the most. I air my load of dirty emotional laundry here to help you identify and analyze your own motives, which will eventually give you the knowledge you need to understand your behavior and that of others. Ultimately, you will learn which strategies work best for you and how a simple Hack or two can make the difference between missing your goals and achieving them.

What is motivation?

We cannot examine our own motivations and behaviors or use a motivational Hack until we agree on what motivation is. The word motivation is derived from the Latin term *movere*, meaning "to move." Technically speaking, any time we invest effort to move toward a goal, we are motivated. In this book, we will define motivation as *the degree of effort and intensity directed toward achieving a goal.* Most motivated behavior can be accelerated or improved—in other words, you can move faster toward your goal—with the motivational Hacks that you will soon master.

Motives have at least two dimensions: *direction* and *intensity.* Direction signifies where we focus our effort. Individuals can aim at a wide variety of outcomes, and different people target their motivated effort in different directions. For example, my effort now is directed toward enhancing your knowledge about motivation. But even when people are directed toward identical outcomes, the effort they invest toward completing the task or meeting the goal fluctuates in intensity. My intensity when writing this book was enormous—I carried my computer everywhere so I could write at a moment's notice. Intensity differences are often the root of motivational conflict between romantic partners, parents and children, and managers and their subordinates. Even people trying to accomplish similar goals have differing priorities about *when* and *how* the goals should be reached.

The motivational Hacks are designed to increase the efficiency of motivated behavior in yourself and others, but the Hacks are useless unless we make accurate assessments about both the direction and intensity of invested effort. If you are highly motivated, aware, and have a compelling reason to make a change, you will learn what it takes to transform your life. Turn to the *Awareness Hacks* (p. 71) now if you are ready to move forward, or instead read my story, where I describe the real game changers in my life and what they meant.

Game Changer 1: *Little Bobby Twist*

Oliver Twist, the main character in the 1830s serial novel by Charles Dickens, was a deviant young orphan boy with questionable morals. Twist did what he must to survive and prosper despite poverty, harsh living conditions, and an unjust social order. Like Twist, I had no clue why I was shipped off to boarding school for third grade, but I clearly remember not wanting to go. The now defunct Nyack Boys School (NBS) was, in my mind, a juvenile detention center, although it was proudly described in the recruiting brochure as a place that provided "a friendly atmosphere which is conducive to natural living and capacity learning." My parents probably wanted little Bobby to thrive in a place with focused teacher attention. Or maybe I was sent away because I was unruly. In second grade, my desk was moved next to that of my teacher, Mrs. Mendelson, facing the class, to keep me under control. Perhaps I needed the structure and discipline that my working parents couldn't supply. My mother, Renee, worked in a doctor's office as a nursing assistant

(this meant I could get vaccinated without an appointment, a questionable benefit from the perspective of an eight-year-old). I knew
that my father, Eugene, was busy fixing broken airplanes for United
Airlines because he came home every day with dirty fingernails and
a fresh supply of airplane barf bags. Renee thought the bags were

Nyack Boys School

an economical way to package my school lunches, since they were free and my cottage cheese wouldn't leak through the bags' plastic lining. This was another bad idea—perhaps not on the same scale as Dwayne the Road King of New Jersey's bridge-busting, but a bad idea nonetheless. Renee's culinary hack gave me my elementary school nickname, *Barf Bag Bobby*. Whatever the reason they sent me to NBS, it made me begin to question other people's wisdom and reasoning and think about *their* motivations.

From the exterior, the school looked inviting, with its Tudor buildings overlooking the majestic Hudson River. There was plenty of school spirit and intramural sports, a school mascot (a Saint Bernard dog), and clean-cut young men dressed in gray pants and navy sport jackets embroidered with the NBS emblem. The inside, however, was more like the famous German prisoner-of-war camp Stalag 17, except with a much lower likelihood of escape. I was surrounded by men in dark suits who referred to each other as "Master." They must have worshiped in the church of discipline, because discipline was all they practiced. They had two kinds of paddles: flat wooden ones for routine beatings, and special ones with little holes drilled in them (holes reduce the air resistance so you can swing faster) that they used for feral boys like me. They had no problem handing out ten whacks if you weren't in bed on time or if you played a prank on one of the other inmates. If you really misbehaved and your bad ass warranted something more than the regular beating, they made you lean up against the wall in your underwear, balancing yourself on the wall with your nose. I had my nose flattened on many occasions, but I surely deserved the nose-flattening I got for leading a conga line of my buddies around the dormitory chanting "Albert is a baby" after poor Albert, one of my classmates, wet his bed for the twentieth time in nineteen nights.

NBS taught me the value of group conformity (p. 120), arbitrary rules, and discipline. If you behaved as the school manifesto dictated, you earned merits and a twenty-five-cent increase in your one-dollar weekly allowance, payable on Saturday morning. If you exercised poor judgment and got caught, you earned demerits, resulting in allowance deductions. But demerits were merely the icing on the conformity cake. All demerits had to be worked off on Saturday mornings, the only day we were released from NBS purgatory. In a gesture of support for local capitalism, we were allowed on Saturday mornings to walk two miles into town to spend money on comics and candy (or for me, a trip to the magic store). But before you could leave, you had to work off your demerits. If you had between one and nine demerits, you had to go to study hall and stand behind a chair, at attention, for nine minutes per demerit before you were released. If you had ten or more demerits, you were really screwed: no allowance, no Saturday morning excursion, and for every demerit over ten, fifteen minutes standing as stiff as the Scarecrow in the Wizard of Oz with a stick up your ass. Thanks, Renee (p. 221).

Was the NBS culture a game changer for me? It is hard to say. I was a handful for sure, someone who generally craved attention. As it turns out, attention-grabbing became a consistent theme for me, and NBS provided many opportunities for me to polish my

Jan 19, 1963

Dear Mom,

How are you? I am fine. Nobody is my friend. I hate every in the school. I might not come home this week end., Everyone is kicking my things around. The school stinks. I have two boxes of pretzils My wacth is brocken

Love,
Bobby

I was not happy back then.

skills. The only way for me to get attention from my parents was by misbehaving, which also earned me personalized attention from faculty and made me the target of many nightly dorm patrols. Living with twelve other nine-year-olds for an entire school year offered plenty of opportunity for creating general mayhem. Ironically, all my behavioral challenges were offset by my stellar academic performance. After a few weeks in the third grade, someone decided I was bored and needed more challenge (p. 102). Apparently, it was not enough that I was separated from my parents, missing my dog Sooty, and could not see my friends back home. It seemed the administrators could not in good conscience ignore the school goal of "capacity learning." Thus, in what appeared to be a joint parental and faculty decision, I was "skipped," moving straight up to the fourth grade.

During this period, decisions made by others were game changers for me, as they are for many children. At the time, skipping a grade seemed great. I became the center of attention and earned a reputation as a boy genius. But nobody (including me) realized that skipping a grade forever positioned me as the youngest, shortest, and dorkiest kid in my class. My circumstances presented many advantages, such as getting noticed by all the girls and piquing the curiosity of my teachers back home. However, children can be cruel, and I remember many years of unsuccessfully trying to fend off bullies with my keen wit and dazzling multiplication skills. The game had clearly changed, especially when I returned home to learn that my parents had divorced.

Game Changer 2: *Latchkey diversions*

Divorce presented all kinds of new opportunities—some good, and others rather disturbing. I returned home for the summer, but I was shipped off to a sleep-away camp for eight weeks. The camp, called Green Chimneys and located in Brewster, New York, was mostly a large open field, where I carried out my main recreational activities: playing softball and frying insects with a magnifying glass.

My desire for attention didn't lessen, but it manifested in a different way at camp. I don't recall having many friends, but one night an accomplice and I devised an ingenious scheme to make sure that all the girls noticed us. (Anonymity was never my strong suit.) The boys were housed in one long dormitory with bunk beds on either side of a central hallway. The girls were segregated in an adjacent building with a similar setup, and connecting doors separated the boys' and girls' quarters. We ran through the girls' dormitory, pulling down any pajama bottoms we could grab, before scurrying off to what we thought was the safety of our dormitory.

We were immediately rounded up, dragged out of our bunk beds, and brought to the center of the girls' dormitory. The camp counselors, who thought our motives were perverted, not prankish (p. 68), surrounded us and stripped us naked. One counselor grabbed each of us by the arms and another held our legs spread apart as the entire camp population gathered around to squawk at our contorting bodies and small genitals while we withered in embarrassment and shame. The humiliation was substantial, and the next thing I remember was my immediate return home. It was on this day that I realized that smart people do stupid things. Surely I did not then have the reasoning ability to understand my own motives, but to this day I still hate pajamas. My camp days were done, and once again my game had been changed.

Fortunately, there are benefits even to a disruptive and unexpected divorce. For one, my mother had to work, which meant I became a latchkey hooligan, home alone for several hours a day after school. It was during these lonely times that I developed and perfected some life-long coping behaviors (p. 126), such as consuming junk food, walking my often-impregnated dog, alphabetizing baseball cards, and watching reruns of *The Three Stooges Show* and *Superman*, shows that starred my role models. Lucky for me, post-divorce austerity meant no money was available to send little Bobby away for institutionalized learning and behavioral control. Instead, I went back to school and lived the life of the average ten-year-old, surviving the fifth and sixth grades by playing the class clown.

Outside of school, my pastimes matched those of my friends in the neighborhood (p. 143). I spent just about all my money on comic books—I knew Murray, the comics delivery guy, because I would wait by the candy store for his weekly arrival. My interest in playing baseball was considerable, but my skills were pathetic. The lack of talent didn't stop me from joining Little League, where my shining accomplishment was getting more walks than anyone else on the team; I was reasonably fast, but I couldn't catch to save my life. I could outwit most of my opponents, though, so I knew when to steal bases and how to take advantage of their frequent attentional lapses. I learned to be strategic by disguising my weaknesses. Miraculously, I was never cut from the team.

Game Changer 3: *Ethnic paranoia*

The calendar turned to 1967 and Renee decided it was time to leave New York City. She was probably motivated by Jewish mother paranoia and by her best friends, Morty and Gert, who had moved to the pastoral suburban community of River Edge, New Jersey. Renee, as a single mother who had lost her own mother when she was fifteen, was quite overprotective. I was not allowed to cross the deserted side street where I lived until I was twelve. Of course, that never stopped me, but getting caught by Renee was something I wanted to avoid. Even back then it was clearly impressed upon me that I should make something of my life (p. 131). She wanted me to have things like a reliable car—one that wasn't in the shop every week—and my own bedroom. She couldn't afford either on her hundred-dollar-a-week paycheck, earned working in the New York City garment center, and the thirty dollars a week my father chipped in for child support. I now realize that she was worried about the massive influx of immigration to our working-class neighborhood and about how these changes would impact me.

Our abrupt departure did save me from the regular beatings I was receiving from the bullies in junior high school. For reasons I didn't understand then, I was crowned *Bagel Boy*, a moniker which did not endear me to gang wannabes who generally hated Jews. I kept score of my defeats by the number of pairs of pants I ripped while assuming the fetal position after getting punched to the ground. Maybe Renee calculated that it was cheaper to move than to constantly go to Robert Hall for new school pants. Despite leaving my lifetime friends, I was happy to move to a swanky one-bedroom apartment in Fort Lee, New Jersey, a suburb of New York City. The apartment overlooked the skyline on the west side of the towering George Washington Bridge, the same bridge I would cross daily in just a few short years. Yes, this was another game changer, this time based on the cultural divide between where I was and where my mother thought I should be.

Game Changer 4: *The unwelcome wagon*

One thing that was the same in New Jersey as in New York was other kids' reactions to me. I was still the shortest kid in the class, still labeled as the brain, and still willing to test the limits of my sarcasm, superhero knowledge, and mediocre athleticism. While waiting for the bus to take me to my first day of junior high, I was approached by a rather robust and jovial fellow wearing gym shorts and bouncing a basketball. Dwayne, the kid who would later become the Road King of Fort Lee, had spotted me standing alone and felt compelled to do his best welcome wagon impersonation. For the next two weeks, Dwayne introduced me to everyone he knew as "Bobby Hoffman, he's in the eighth grade." He never just used my name. I appreciated his kindness, but I felt like I was his science fair project. The pressure was on. The Smart Kid label felt visible on my forehead, like an exploding zit, and I felt compelled to meet other people's expectations, although their standards made me anxious and resistant (p. 120).

I was immediately put to the test. Between my December birthday and my skipping third grade, I was almost two years younger than many of my classmates. I was naïve compared to my eighth-grade peers, and I clearly lacked the flooding hormones of my teenage comrades. I was interested in sports and survival while most of my buddies were busy dreaming about boobs. Most everyone except Dwayne noticed I was a bit unusual. I clearly remember my first New Jersey school confrontation; I was bluntly quizzed by two Scott Farkas lookalikes who asked, "Hey, new boy, what's a cocksucker?" I immediately replied with feigned confidence, "It's a bird, you morons," and dashed away. From that day forward I was labeled (p. 55) as a dweeb, and I realized that my adolescent education had begun. I quickly found that different cultures sometimes shared customs; New Jersey kids were just as cruel as the New York bastards that had wrecked so many pairs of my pants. Luckily, Dwayne also had a rather lackluster reputation, a basketball, some dorky friends, a three-foot stack of Playboy magazines, and plenty of energy—essentials that comforted both of us.

Game Changer 5: *Teenage wasteland*

As the years went by, I learned many more lessons, most of them outside of school. For example, I realized my mother had interests beyond me, because she started going out much more when I entered high school. Little did I know that Renee had a well-designed plan (p. 174) for her future and mine that included finding a rich husband to support us. Her prospecting created a wealth of opportunities for her to enjoy fancy dinners with potential suitors. It also developed my neighborhood reputation as a convivial host, because I had something that most teenagers craved: a place to go without adult supervision—a teenage treehouse (minus the tree). Our first-floor apartment became a gathering place for my friends to hang out, and we played poker every day after school. As time passed, I developed my social skills, courtesy of Dwayne's tutelage and lessons from other kids in my apartment building. My apartment became the location of choice for high school kids to smoke pot, listen to music, and (rarely) entertain not-so-innocent girls.

To support my poker habit and maintain my hospitable reputation, I needed income. I was always willing to work hard—I had been delivering newspapers since I turned thirteen—and my career prospects exploded at fifteen, when I landed the coveted position of dry cleaning delivery boy. Fort Lee, New Jersey, as a suburb of New York City, was mostly high-rise apartments that needed amenities to attract residents. Just about all the apartments had "valets," a fancy name for places where you drop off your dirty laundry. Lucky for me, someone had to return the clean clothes, and I was uniquely qualified, having done my own laundry for years. I earned a dollar per hour, plus tips, and worked two hours a day after school and Saturdays. It was a position of some status, and I gained some valuable skills during my tenure that would come in handy for many more years.

The real fringe benefit of this job was my boss, Alan, a long-haired hippie freak who always seemed to have women hanging around the back room of the valet office. But it wasn't Alan's diminutive stature or his Frank Zappa–style Fu Manchu moustache that was attracting the girls: it was his reefer supply. While I was in the front smelling dirty laundry, Alan and friends were in the back getting stoned. Even though I was generally known to be awkward with the ladies, I was a typical teenager, hormonal and love deprived, and I admired Alan's girlfriend Jackie, who was a beautiful, girl-next-door blonde, all personality and charm. Alan knew I liked Jackie. After smoking a few bowls, Alan thought it would be amusing to watch his dorky virginal assistant give Jackie a kiss, and she agreed to the bizarre proposition. I was reluctant to be Alan's circus act, but I succumbed to the pressure and launched myself toward Jackie with the force of projectile vomit. I jackhammered a kiss on her sexy lips while giving her right boob my best mammogram impression. She screamed in pain and horror, Alan laughed until he fell off his chair, and I learned a few lessons. Social motivation suddenly became much more important (p. 128), but once again I felt humiliated—although I definitely learned how *not* to give a kiss.

The rest of high school was consumed with the typical teenage distractions of the 1970s: hanging out in the local park drinking Boone's Farm Apple Wine or smoking pot, playing basketball, and

16 and graduated

listening to classic rock (we just called it "rock"). Sixteen arrived too soon, and it was time to graduate from high school. The good news was that I finally grew to 5'10" and Renee convinced a rich, bald, Napoleonic sausage vendor with a big house to marry her. The bad news was that I moved to Paramus, New Jersey, about ten miles away from my teenage home.

The move meant I took frequent bus rides or hitchhiked to see my friends, unless I could bribe one of them to pick me up. The really deflating news was that I had to make the first pseudo-adult decision of my life. Graduation meant working full-time or going to college. Working meant being bored at 7-Eleven or at one of my other part-time jobs (delivering phonebooks, selling greeting cards door to door, or watering plants at the local flower shop). But my domineering Jewish mother wouldn't settle for a job; she forced me to go to college, hoping that one day her son would be a doctor. From Renee's viewpoint, it would be sacrilegious to skip college and spend my life laboring in a blue-collar job, a fate that was highly contrary to her beliefs (p. 128), although she herself lacked a formal college education.

Game Changer 6: *Double secret probation*

I begrudgingly enrolled at the school closest to my new home, Fairleigh Dickinson University (FDU). Although it was the largest institution in New Jersey, the obscure school was affectionately known to locals as Fairly Ridiculous, the embarrassing place you went when no better options were available. I declared a major in psychology, but I had no authentic interest in academics or anything else. My life was a mess. I was too young to drive; I needed a job; and I desperately wanted a girlfriend so I could leverage my debonair romantic experience with Jackie. To make matters worse, the sausage vendor, whose real name is too despicable to repeat, forced me to unload his truck of unsold salamis and bolognas every night, conscripting me into work to pay for my rent-free room in his house. Sausage Man was on a quest to evict me as quickly as he could without pissing off his new bride.

I surely needed some motivational Hacks back then. No one told me that freedom of choice was important for strong task commitment (p. 140). Maybe if I had felt like I had choices about school, I would have invested more effort into studying. Unlike high school, where I could just show up and get A's and B's, it took me an entire year of college to realize that it was the effort invested, not ability (p. 224), that was the key to academic success. But I spent too much time that first semester huddled in a phone booth across the street from the university, smoking pot between classes, which in turn meant that I often spent afternoons playing pinball in the Student Union instead of in class. Also, it was a really bad idea to skip biology lab until the fifth week of the semester. But that's what happens when you have spent your entire life being told you are a "brain." It wasn't until many years later that I would learn that overconfidence constrains effort (p. 82). My perception of intellectual superiority was shattered when I ended my first year at FDU with a whopping 1.67 GPA, an average I achieved by failing both Spanish *and* English. I did, however, develop some excellent forgery skills that year, erasing the embarrassing report-card grades and replacing them with A's and B's. I was not going to let Renee find out I screwed up.

After that first semester, something happened that changed the course of my entire life. I don't know why, but I decided to take control of my future (p. 114). Maybe it was because I was growing up, maybe it was because of sheer embarrassment and social pressure (p. 87), or maybe it was because I realized hauling sausages for a psychopath stepfather was a crummy lifestyle. I was studying psychology and learning about how people think (mostly because I wanted to learn how to make girls like me), and this led to some deeper self-exploration. I experienced the textbook Freudian catharsis. The light bulb went off. I had mystical revelations *without* pot. I curbed my phone booth visits and found a girlfriend. I realized I was not like anyone else, and I didn't care! I was still concerned about meeting expectations (p. 120) and embarrassed about my grades, but I realized that change was a choice—something I controlled. I committed to turning my academic career around for my own personal gain, but I also realized something else that would change the game for the rest of my life.

For the first time, I began to question the status quo (p. 209). I wanted to know why I thought differently than the rest of the

My 1970s hair (L)—with one of the gang

world. I deeply pondered why my Fort Lee friends were making the choices they were making—why some quit college and others couldn't live up to simple commitments like showing up for a date. I was especially puzzled by why I could learn to exercise self-control (p. 189) and curb my pot-smoking while others struggled to quit but indulged even more. Of course, like many people, I thought my way of thinking and my choices were better than others' (p. 57)— not in an absolute sense, but in terms of making the most out of whatever talent and potential I had. I wondered why my friends had different priorities than I did, why they seemed unable to take control of their lives, why they were so vulnerable to social pressure. I could not figure out why people made their choices and acted the way they did, and I was committed to finding the answer one way or another.

Game Changer 7: *I have nunchuck skills*

When I graduated from FDU I landed a job at a photo lab. In the days before Facebook and Instagram, to see your pictures, you had to send film to a place to get them printed. The lab hired me without hesitation, perhaps because I had spent my undergraduate years working for a family friend as a photographer's assistant and darkroom zombie developing black-and-white film. Or perhaps it was because I was willing to work any day of the week, at any time, for the twenty-four-hour operation. What shocked me was they didn't ask me any questions. No "tell us about a time when you worked on a team." No "What is a skill you want to refine?" No "Can you juggle four cucumbers while riding a unicycle?" *Nothing.*

My lab experience was a definite game changer—their inept hiring practices triggered my decision to go to graduate school and get a master's degree in human resources psychology. The decision meant I would spend the better part of three years studying the application of psychological principles to working environments in order to create greater productivity and efficiency in organizations. I was interested in management and leadership—I wanted to boss people around after all the crap I endured growing up in New York City. So the mess at the Union Photo Company in Clifton, New Jersey, turned out to be one of the primary influences in my life for the next twenty years. As for the actual job, I worked there for five years and learned the photo-manufacturing business. The mindlessness of the job allowed me to use my skill and moxie to devise a plan that would change my future motivations and what I accomplished for the rest of my life.

After graduate school, I was making six-fifty an hour, feeling useless and underemployed. I had paid for my grad school tuition by working weekends as a taxi driver and as an ID checker at a local bar in Fort Lee, in addition to my job at the lab. The taxi gig frequently brought me to Manhattan and gave me the chance to act insane, like Robert De Niro in *Taxi Driver,* an extremely popular movie in 1976. At the bar, I could drink for free and perform noble deeds like kicking out underage drinkers (one of the people I kicked out was Toni, the girl that would eventually become my ex-wife). Despite these perks, I needed a better job.

Renee had already had enough of the Sausage Man, who by this time was throwing apple cores in the toilet just to aggravate her. I was finished with school, so she no longer had to tolerate his abuse to help me. I felt compelled to make something happen for her and for me, and adversity stimulates growth. While I had never felt especially creative, I had also never been in a situation where I needed to be resourceful (p. 108). I reached a decision: since I couldn't find a job, I'd create one for myself. Then all my problems would be solved! Or so I thought.

The only person that was tighter with money than the Sausage Man was Robert Rachesky, the man who owned the Union Photo family business. After trying to find a job for about six months, it occurred to me that I could parlay my photo lab knowledge into a full-time job if I could convince Rachesky to invest in me. After trying multiple times over two weeks to get an appointment, we finally met, and he agreed to my proposal: I would conduct an organizational analysis of Union Photo. This was primarily designed to showcase my skills, but my plan would also save Rachesky money—clearly a primary motivation (p. 160) for him, based upon how he ran the company. We had a deal. Rachesky would get inside business intelligence from me, and if I was successful, I would get a title and some badly needed human resources experience.

For the next few months, I wrote some generally well-received reports for Union Photo. My first post-graduate project was titled "Morale and Motivation: A Report to the President" (fairly ironic, given the state of my own morale and motivation at the time). My narrative addressed the topics of employee wellness, productivity, and positive employee relations. I don't know what appealed to Rachesky, but he bought into my plan; now it came down to negotiating a deal with someone that could coax nickels out of Scrooge. Maybe I undersold myself, but I proposed a deal where my hourly salary would be multiplied by forty hours and converted to a weekly paycheck. My plea included the ballsy admission that "due to my lack of professional corporate experience you should consider this proposal to be a bargain." In return, I would get the title Personnel Manager, valuable experience, and an office conveniently adjacent

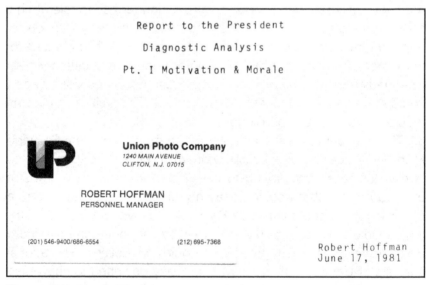

The report that landed the job

to the plant where my then—love interest worked. He agreed. Game changer.

Game Changer 8: *Dumped*

Over the next seven months, I accomplished quite a bit in my new management role. I alienated all my former coworkers, enraged a union representative (whom I had formerly supported in contract negotiations) so much that he leaped across the bargaining table to choke me, and became so arrogant and obnoxious that my office girlfriend dumped me. While none of these outcomes particularly disturbed me, the job turned out to be less than satisfying, because I felt powerless and poor. About this time, I had two other moti-vational game-changing experiences. First, one rainy Hanukkah night in December of 1981, Sausage Man and Renee got into a terrible argument. While I wasn't what they were battling over, he knew that Renee would only put up with his antics and abuse until I moved out, and he wanted a divorce. From my mother's viewpoint, my moving out meant moving into my own apartment. In the mind of the Salami Schmuck, it meant kicking the kid out on the street so his wife would leave too. Midway through the battle royale, the doorbell rang and the police arrived. Sausage Prick told the police I was trespassing and should be removed from the house, although I had been paying him rent since I finished grad school.

I had fifteen minutes to pack my clothes and my important pos-sessions (my bong and patchouli incense), and boom: I never slept there again. From his perspective, mission accomplished! From my perspective, homelessness! Luckily, I had been dating Toni, the girl who I kicked out of the bar a few months earlier. Her compassionate parents and many of my Fort Lee friends allowed me to couch-surf, sleeping at their homes until I could find a permanent place to live, but those first few months were miserable. I never knew where I would sleep; I sometimes wound up in roach-infested discount motels where people could rent rooms by the hour. However, adversity stimulated growth once again. Within two months I had secured a new job; a few months later, I married Toni, then a Marie Osmond lookalike (her father had once angrily chased me around his dining room table until I agreed to set a wedding date; I married her anyway).

My new job at ORBA had many of the perks aspiring young graduates wanted in the opulent eighties. I had a comfortable salary, an office in a futuristic oblong glass building, a glamorous secretary, and a staff of people I could boss around; this felt right to me, with my poorly calibrated perceptions of my own ability (p. 82). My new boss Jim and I got along famously—so well that we had lunch together daily. Developmentally, I was immersed in a profitable business and learning the material handling industry, which focused on engineering and building storage facilities for energy resources. While I wasn't enthused about coal and oil storage, I *was* enamored with my position, the fancy suits I wore, and my responsibilities. I was part of a highly functioning team for the first time, and I engaged in my work to such an extent that after working there for only a few months I invited my boss and the entire staff to our wedding. For the first time in my working career, I felt committed to the organization where I worked and took pride in the success of those around me (p. 143).

One day at ORBA I learned a very important lesson about priorities and perspectives. The president of the company was a middle-aged Chinese gentleman, Dr. Yu, who reminded me of the James Bond villain Dr. No: tall, thin, aloof, and mysterious. Jim always referred to him as Toby when we met privately, but outside of his office, no one would dare call our leader anything but Dr. Yu. I figured he was most likely a PhD with some sort of engineering degree. He generally seemed demanding and curt, rarely speaking to anyone but his direct reports, but one day he asked me to mail a package to China. Back in those days, overseas delivery took up to a week, even with the advent of the newly formed Federal Express Company. Since Dr. Yu made his request to me at four o'clock p.m., when the mailroom employee I supervised was already gone for the day, I left the package on my desk to send the next morning. In retrospect, this small act of corporate naïveté probably cost me my job. About four weeks later, the day I returned to work after my two-week honeymoon, my good buddy Jim told me I was being laid off. From this game changer, I learned that there are differences in motivation across people (p. 53), and other people's priorities might not match your own beliefs. Clearly, although I didn't give a crap about Dr. Yu's package or about China, he did. Getting dumped had benefits, though—after ORBA, I learned some important life skills, including how to play golf and collect unemployment benefits.

The year following my premature departure from ORBA was a nightmare. After about six months of marriage, I realized I'd made a terrible mistake when in a fit of rage my charming bride destroyed my prized plant, a *Dieffenbachia*, which had been a gift to commemorate my first apartment. Long before the wedding, my mother had warned me that I wouldn't be happy and that my marriage would fail. Of course, I disagreed with her at the time; I was emotionally engaged and wasn't able to think logically (p. 74). Toni was Italian Catholic and I was not. For some reason, though, I discounted our cultural differences in the name of love, ample breasts, and the fact that I didn't care much about religion.

My decision to get married in church caused tidal waves of cultural tension, and Renee would not speak to me for several months. After threatening not to attend, she showed up at the wedding at the last second and made a rather noticeable entry to the church, stealing the show with her flamboyant dress. Even Father Peter, the priest, paused mid-sentence as Renee ambled up to the front pew with her wealthy new Italian boyfriend Ben, twenty-five years her senior. The wedding celebration was glorious, capped by the traditional mother-son dance, during which Renee gently whispered in my ear, "You have made the biggest mistake of your life." Too bad I didn't realize back then just how accurate her foresight was. Thanks, Renee.

Besides my matrimonial malcontent, my career was stagnant; I spent most of my time answering ads and collecting rejection letters (this was before the job search was reduced to keyword compatibility). I was beginning to doubt my own efficacy (p. 95) and question my skills. I was driving a taxi, which at least kept me

Wedding day. Dad and Renee, long divorced, agreed to pose.

busy during the exhaustive job search, but I wondered if I would be a cabbie for the rest of my life. Finally, ten months after villainous Dr. Yu altered my destiny (p. 114), I landed a human resources position at the Alco-Gravure Company in Hoboken, New Jersey. Alco was a nationwide hundred-year-old business that specialized in printing color magazine sections for newspapers and advertisers. At Alco, I began to understand the value of multiculturalism and teamwork—not from a racial or status perspective, but because different people have different priorities and will ardently defend their personal beliefs (p. 90) when they must. The guys in Memphis liked barbeque and beer, the folks in Los Angeles were into sushi, and the employees of the Chicago plant loved to talk about kielbasa, their families, and bowling. Each group and culture was vastly different, but we all wanted the same things: autonomy to do our jobs, respect for what we accomplished, and team comradery (p. 143). It didn't matter how much I had learned in school; I was just now learning about the most important things in life.

My Alco experience helped me grow in several other ways. By the time I left the company for a higher-paying job in 1985, I had amassed a nice portfolio of stock. The company was employee owned, meaning that every year employees accrued shares of stock based on salary. My self-esteem was at an all-time high from the sophistication (self-assessed, of course) (p. 82) I'd gained from my Alco lifestyle. It was my job to entertain people at fancy restaurants and social gatherings in major U.S. cities after industry meetings, training seminars, and plant location visits, all on the company expense account. On any given night, I could be found at the finest steakhouse in town, boosting my ego and elevating my cholesterol while amusing my coworkers or clients. Although I grew both personally and professionally during these years, I was still dissatisfied. I wanted more, and it wasn't until one night in December 1984 that I learned *more* would happen with *less*.

One meeting brought me to the posh Opryland Hotel in Nashville, Tennessee. Home to the finest in country music, the sprawling hotel and entertainment complex was quite an attraction for the first-time visitor. As usual, several employees came along for the company-funded socializing. On this occasion, our meeting ended on Friday afternoon. Having worked all week with no chance to explore the local clubs and music venues, I decided to stay an extra night. I figured I had earned a little out-of-town revelry by being a good corporate soldier all week long. After a long night of drinking and dancing, I returned to my room at two o'clock a.m. to the insistent blinking of the red message light on the phone. Gert, my

Renee at her post-divorce best

mother's old friend from New York, had left six voice messages instructing me to call her no matter what time I returned. It was bad news.

The months following Renee's death from a heart attack at age fifty-one were turbulent for me. As her only child, I made all the funeral arrangements and buried her. I inherited her assets—bills from Bloomingdale's, a thirty-five-piece hat collection, the rundown 12-cylinder Jaguar she was awarded in the divorce, a broken Rolex watch, a gauche three-carat diamond ring that looked like a fly's head, and a cashed-out whole-life insurance policy. The bill collectors called daily, and kept calling even after the "I'm so sorry" calls from friends and relatives had stopped. I also inherited plenty of guilt. Renee and I had an argument just before I left for Nashville, and we had not spoken the week of her death. I blamed the Sausage Dick for her early demise, since he had put her through the most horrendous divorce possible, cutting off her health insurance to make her suffer and fabricating income tax returns to reduce his alimony. I decided to move into her apartment. Toni resisted this, as she did most things I proposed (except marriage), but Renee's influence on me did not end when she died—it actually increased. I was about to turn thirty and thought it was a good time to stop focusing on self-indulgence and personal pleasure and start acting like a responsible adult. Immediately, I put my plan into action (p. 157).

Game Changer 9: *The hard way*

After Renee's death, my behaviors radically changed. Toni and I had fought for years about the fact that I wasn't ready for children. I thought children would interfere with my plan for global domination and massive wealth accumulation. Now, I began to think that having a child would cement my mother's legacy and carry the Hoffman name to the next generation. Within fifteen months of Renee's death, Toni gave birth to a bouncing baby boy. We named him Robert in honor of Renee, following the Jewish tradition of naming a newborn after a deceased family member. Robert's first act was to pee on both me and the doctor. I should have known then he would be a handful. At the same time, I decided to improve my health. I began a daily workout regime and started running. I quit smoking both cigarettes and weed. I landed a new, higher-paying human resources job with a subsidiary of American Express. Suddenly, my priorities and commitments changed, and I developed a tenacious focus that would last for the next twenty-five years.

For the first five years after Renee's death, my resurgent energy and focused attention resulted in measurable accomplishments. Exercising daily helped build my strength. Running four or five times

Father and son

a week increased my stamina and tested the limits of my endur-
ance. I had incredible energy, and it paid off in many ways. During
my time with American Express, the company divested from "non-
essential" operations, including the insurance business, Fireman's
Fund, where I was working. The divestiture meant opportunity. I
was promoted several times; I eventually had leadership responsibility for almost a thousand employees in eight offices across six
states, and I directly supervised a team of ten. My physical confidence soared. I regularly entered 5K and 10K races, running with
one goal in mind, to best my past performance (p. 87). Although
I never won any medals, I did surpass many of my peers, completed
a half-marathon, and earned a reputation for being willing to try anything to test and improve my skills. I felt like I was finally controlling
my destiny (p. 114), a belief that developed over time as I realized that hard work and dedicated effort produce results (p. 224).

Successful as I was, I still yearned for something more, and kept thinking that one day I might go back to school to earn my PhD.

I had been commuting twenty-five miles a day to my insurance job for several years. To shorten my commute and to give my children the best lifestyle I could afford, we moved to the upscale community of Mountain Lakes, New Jersey. The local school system was extraordinary. It had a 100 percent high school graduation rate and a 97 percent college acceptance rate, and despite Toni's opposition, I felt sure that the new location was best for three-year-old Rebecca and for Robert, who was then entering the second grade. As the family breadwinner, I made the unilateral decision to relocate. Unfortunately, right about the time we moved, my job at the insurance company was eliminated. *Carpe diem.* A game changer of monumental proportions was about to happen, but not quite yet.

It was about this time that I began contemplating going into business on my own. At first, consulting was a slow and frustrating grind. I spent my limited money on stamps, printing, and materials (back then, people were still excited to receive snail mail). I landed a few gigs with local companies, but nothing substantial—certainly not enough to pay the inflated Mountain Lakes mortgage. My job search was relentless. I attended every networking meeting I could find, presenting myself as confident and informed, but inside I was anxious and worried (p. 146) about my unemployment benefits running out. Although I conducted occasional seminars, I was still broke, and I needed to go back to school or find some other way to make money. I answered an advertisement for a director of human resources job at a small but growing firm on Wall Street named CBD. While the opportunity to work in New York City seemed glamorous and exciting, it also meant paying additional taxes and commuting expenses, as well as enduring a daily commute of three hours or more.

I put on my best suit and left my house at six o'clock a.m. for a twenty-mile drive to the train station, where I boarded a train that went through the World Trade Center. I then took a cab to Wall Street, where I arrived for my interview at eight o'clock a.m.

I waited for almost two hours before I was interviewed. The initial interview, with the company's chief financial officer, went well. My prospective boss, Steven Trellis, seemed like a friendly, affable guy—a George Costanza type, but taller and with less hair. Trellis must have been interested, because for the next eight hours I was tossed around the office like a bowl of jelly beans. Everyone with any prominence told me how I could help the company grow and why it was such a great place to work. At about six o'clock p.m., I was brought back to the lobby and asked to wait for Trellis to come get me. About an hour later, Trellis brought me into his office and offered me $80,000 a year with a $5,000 signing bonus—far more money than I had ever earned in a job. Trellis said he needed my decision immediately. This made me suspicious—I had never heard of a company making an on-the-spot offer without checking references—but I was in no position to decline (p. 74). I started work the next day.

I can only describe the CBD culture as ruthless and abusive. I was too naïve at the time to realize it, but it wasn't my skills that appealed to Trellis—it was my unemployment and my financial vulnerability. The salary was nothing more than hazard pay, and I would soon come to regret taking it. In many ways, the company felt more like an organized crime business than a legitimate enterprise: people came and went, turf battles were neverending, verbal sparring and arguments were unsuccessfully muffled by closed doors—something was *always* amiss, and everyone knew it. Most nights I wasn't allowed to leave until eight or nine o'clock p.m. His Excellency, King Trellis, gave me dirty looks when I departed before seven o'clock p.m. The only thing more disturbing than Trellis's temperament was his vocabulary. His wrath fell upon everyone at CBD at some point, but as his direct report, I was subjected to regular tongue-lashings when his orders weren't followed down to the most trivial detail.

One day he asked me to force some employees to move from their current space to a smaller, more crowded part of the office. I deferred the move until I could talk to the president of the affected employees' division, wanting to promote harmony between the divisions. When Trellis learned that I'd delayed the move, he called me into his messy office with its mountains of files and piles of paperwork covering his desk. When I told him why I'd done it, he screamed, *"I told you to move those fucking assholes out yesterday! What's wrong with you?"* He followed up with a full-circle Sandy-Koufax-level windup to an arm sweep across the desk. Every single piece of paper and the telephone crashed to the floor. I told Trellis we would finish the conversation later and walked out. It was my thirty-eighth birthday and almost Christmas Eve, and I wanted to get home before midnight.

The CBD debacle came to a head during the spring of '94. While conducting employee benefit meetings, I deliberately disobeyed Trellis. As part of a benefit plan conversion, he wanted me to advise employees to invest their 401(k) assets into a shoddy investment plan run by one of his buddies. While finance wasn't my forte, the motivation for the change seemed sketchy at best. After I conducted the first meeting, Trellis told me I should be more persuasive in influencing where and how employees invested their prior 401(k) contributions, which in some cases amounted to several hundred thousand dollars. According to established federal law, my role as a plan fiduciary obligated me to uphold the federal regulations covering employee benefit plans while providing employees with unbiased information and not unduly influencing their investment decisions.

Trellis couldn't care less about my ethical obligations. He warned me to conduct the remaining meetings the way he wanted or it would be a big problem for both of us. To avoid another Trellis temper tantrum, I agreed, but I lied. I wasn't about to conform to his twisted demands. I conducted the next meeting the same as I had the first. It was only a matter of time before Trellis found out that I had disobeyed his orders. I waited for a call from Trellis as I boarded my flight to L.A. with my longtime friend and investment advisor Reagan Ford, who was accompanying me to conduct the Los Angeles meetings. We settled into our first-class seats and made our escape from New York before Trellis found out that his dastardly plan had been foiled.

We knew we were heading for a Wild West–style ambush. When we arrived at the Casa del Mar, our elegant 1920s beach-front hotel, the desk clerk handed me a message that read "DO NOT CONDUCT ANY MORE MEETINGS. RETURN TO NEW YORK IMMEDIATELY. Trellis." Ford and I pondered our predicament and the meetings scheduled for the following morning with the Los Angeles staff. After downing a few martinis, we decided to ignore the note and go to the local office the following morning. When we arrived, the local VP was waiting to inform us that the meeting had been cancelled. I was instructed to call Trellis, who told me I was fired for insubordination. Since our return flight wasn't for another two days, Ford and I elected to stay. It was like a scene from a John Grisham novel—we were constantly looking around, feeling as if we were being followed and that any moment could be our last. We had two days of sunburn, paranoia, and inebriation before the flight back to New York and a meeting with Trellis the next morning. He offered me six months of salary, executive outplacement, and a positive reference in exchange for a signed agreement that included a gag order prohibiting me from ever disclosing the details of my termination and of that tumultuous year at CBD.

Bucking Trellis was probably the easiest decision I ever made, despite its potentially grave consequences. Perhaps I should have feared the unknown, but I felt comfortable with my decision and confident about my future. I walked out of CBD mostly unscathed, with my ethics intact and $40,000 in my pocket. I felt again like I was in control of my destiny (p. 114). I had been paid off because I refused to compromise my beliefs: it was unconscionable and unethical to deliberately deceive my coworkers. I had no job, but I realized that I actually had *more* security. Now I could rely on myself and invest my time and effort into developing my consulting business without the distraction of full-time employment. Working for myself, I would be less vulnerable to the whims of a distant corporate executive or a maniacal boss. If I failed, it was my fault—there would be no one to blame. I felt liberated. Getting fired was the best thing that ever happened to me. Trellis's campaign for power and control taught me a valuable lesson, one that I couldn't have learned in any school.

Game Changer 10: *Funny money*

The next ten years were a period of remarkable growth for me. I learned new industries while working with over thirty organizations, including Fortune 500 companies in the entertainment, media, pharmaceutical, accounting, and global finance businesses and dozens of small entrepreneurial and internet start-up companies. I worked on the set of *Saturday Night Live*, in the office of former NBA Commissioner Larry Stern, and down the hall from General Electric leadership icon Jack Welch. I gained new skills by modeling myself on the successful executives who hired me at rates of up to $200 per hour. I staffed global organizations, created career development programs, and redesigned departments. When I worked at 30 Rockefeller Center, I was accidentally knocked to the floor by a newsroom door swung open by *Today Show* weatherman Al Roker before he lost a hundred pounds. On another occasion, I was thrown off the set of the *Rosie O'Donnell Show* for talking above a whisper. And my new lifestyle allowed me to work from home: I volunteered in my children's classes, chaperoned field trips to Fairy Tale Forest and the Bronx Zoo, and attended school recitals and the annual Mountain Lakes Halloween parade. I called the shots, worked when I wanted, and even took my family on business trips. Life was good.

My game-changing break did not materialize until I was contacted by a friend who was working as a consultant for GE Capital, the billion-dollar finance business of the General Electric Corporation and one of the largest and most profitable banking institutions on the planet. GE was then one of the top companies in the world in which to gain leadership experience because of mastermind Jack Welch's legendary leadership. The core values of the organization included being held accountable, treating people with respect by giving them candid feedback, and running the business like you

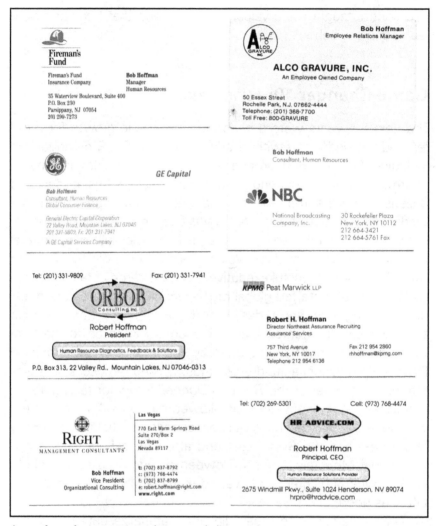

Just a few of my many employers and clients

owned it. GE was a game changer for me because the messages embedded in the GE culture deeply influenced my personal development and evolving beliefs—more than any other organization I had encountered. Colleagues valued my contributions, gave recognition when I deserved it, and embraced me as part of the team. Most importantly, the leaders modeled the type of values and ethics they described in their glossy brochures. At GE, if someone said they would do something, it would be done and done right. For these reasons (and the outrageous pay), I consulted for GE for five years.

But GE wasn't my only client during this period. In the nineties, money and opportunities were so prevalent that I had to decide which jobs to accept and which to decline. The late nineties had the highest rate of business expansion in the previous sixty years, primarily fueled by the explosive growth of fledgling dot-com businesses. Companies like Amazon, eBay, Yahoo, and AOL were just beginning to emerge as business innovators. Personally, Toni and I were tolerating each other because the extra money allowed us each to do our own thing. We had new cars, took vacations, and catered to the whims of our children. I bought a Jaguar and thousand-dollar suits, and I plowed plenty of money into stocks, which were skyrocketing as newly formed companies came to market and doubled their stock prices in a day. My phone wouldn't stop ringing. Sometimes I was so busy I billed clients for sixteen hours a day, and I had to be productive and efficient—to do more than what my clients expected. But I still wasn't satisfied; I didn't really care about the money because I wasn't happy. It took several years, but my idea that money could be a motivator slowly disappeared. Despite the outward appearance of success (p. 146), I was troubled, bored, and restless. I knew I needed more.

Game Changer 11: *"He's not moving"*

Almost overnight, my world and the lives of others around me crashed. On March 10, 2000, the NASDAQ stock exchange peaked at 5,132.52. Within two years, the exchange lost over 60 percent of its value—more than a five-trillion-dollar loss in company valuations. Less than eighteen months later, the 9/11 terrorist attacks on the United States further deteriorated the economic climate and pushed the country into a new protective ideology. For most organizations, growth and expansion were fond memories. The culture and economics of business changed. The high-flying days of inflated salaries for temporary employees and consultants, retention incentives, and $20K signing bonuses were over. Personally, my financial losses were minimal, but like most people, I felt ripple effects from the bursting of the dot-com bubble—the primary reason for the economic downturn. GE issued a new edict that consultants could not work for more than twelve consecutive months. My old buddy Reagan, who had employed me after the CBD adventure, sold his business and eliminated my role. Many of my other clients were approaching retirement or moving to companies that did not employ contractual workers. I was in trouble.

In the winter of 2001, I finally decided to return to school, but I wasn't sure what to study or where to go. I decided to attend the University of Nevada, Las Vegas (UNLV), and study educational psychology, a field closely related to training and development that focuses on the psychology of how people learn, think, and are motivated. I closed the deal when my prospective advisor, Dr. Gale Sinatra, offered me free tuition and a stipend of $20,000 per academic year (although I was used to earning ten times that). My grad student servitude would require me to work twenty hours a week supporting two professors as a graduate assistant. I suspected I would have to learn how to conduct research while making tons of photocopies. It seemed simple—I would essentially be paid to go to school and earn a degree. I thought I could work part-time in a Vegas bar or casino to earn extra money while I secured my future as a prominent professor.

I went back home to announce the decision to my family. Predictably, Toni balked. She was now thoroughly used to the Mountain Lakes lifestyle of well-manicured lawns and sprawling lakefront mansions, and she wanted to stay in New Jersey. The kids were indifferent, but the Las Vegas mystique sparked some mild curiosity. Robert was finishing high school and Rebecca had yet to reach her blossoming social potential; from my perspective, the timing was ideal. I was planning (p. 165) and taking action before my income dried up. I knew it would be hard work for me and an upheaval for the family, but the risk versus return calculation (p. 105) justified my decision. We boarded an airplane to shop for a house and found the perfect location. As Toni and I discussed the move in our room at the Las Vegas Hard Rock Hotel, Rebecca went down the hall to get some ice. She returned trembling, swearing there was a dead body in the hallway. We were skeptical at first—she was a dramatic child—but I gave an obligatory glance down the corridor. Two doors away there was a gurney with a motionless figure draped in a white sheet. We turned on the news to learn that John Entwistle, the bassist for the legendary rock band The Who, had mysteriously passed away after a night of sleeping with a stripper. Ironically, that was also the day my marriage died, as Toni unilaterally decided that I would relocate to Las Vegas alone. Entwistle wasn't moving, but I told Rebecca I was. She cried.

   I sacrificed my charmed life for two reasons. First, my sense of how important money was had changed over the years. I now

In memory of John Entwistle

believed that money was made to be spent. I had built a solid nest egg over ten years of hard work, always knowing in the back of my mind that I would need savings to carry me through my return to school as a full-time student. Although grad school would create a short-term earnings drought, I was securing my future and deliberately putting myself in a position where I would be cognitively challenged. Second, I wanted to model responsible adult behavior for my children. I had never felt confident about my parenting abilities. Both my children had adolescent escapades (I'll leave it to Rebecca to tell those stories), and neither was especially motivated by academics. Toni and I constantly fought over how to raise them. We both wanted to teach them proper values, good habits, and respect, but we rarely agreed on methods. The kids learned early on how to pit us against each other. I was the disciplinarian with little tolerance for misbehavior or for lack of effort. Their mother had different

---

Dearest Rebecca:

Tonight, you said this is the last time for a bedtime kiss and I told you, "things will work out for the best and we will be better off when I am finished with school." The reality of my leaving is that I will lose much, but gain as well. Right now, it seems the loss is greater, as I will miss you so much. The most difficult part of leaving will be when I cannot see you smile, pout, goof around, make funny words and just do the things you do. Most of all, I will miss kissing you goodnight and the daily hugs when I see you.

These may be tough times for us all, but remember, I am doing this so all of us will be happier in the future. What makes it really difficult is spending so much time together in the last few weeks of our trip. Just think of all the memories we can talk about for years to come.

You are the most wonderful daughter anyone could ask for. I will think of you all the time and be counting the days until I can come home. Make sure you don't change your ways, and take good care of Mommy while I am gone.

All My Love,

Daddy

Daddy
August 17, 2002

A very tough decision

beliefs—she was the nurturing, caring, emotionally comforting parent. Even when Robert used the two-inch space between his bed and his bedroom wall as a trash can, leaving a year's worth of candy wrappers melting on the baseboard, Toni's temper was unscathed.

Yelling was my norm, shouting expectations and cursing like a Russian dictator. I reflected on the time when I forced my son to run alongside me for ten miles on a hot summer afternoon, or the time I went berserk when my daughter bought a canary while I was away on a business trip. I had always left my expertise in performance management and feedback at the office and acted like a grumpy dad. I hoped that my decision to give up everything to improve myself over the long term would speak much louder than any of my former words. I wanted to show the children that under any circumstances, at any age, we could reverse our fortunes, make sacrifices, and accomplish our goals. I wanted to set a better example and hopefully make up for my child-rearing mistakes of the prior years. The game changed once more.

Game Changer 12: *Déjà vu*

I thought that my twenty years of working in the top echelon of the corporate world meant I knew how things worked. But I quickly discovered that I didn't know much about academia. I assumed professors taught, then went home to drink wine and have big thoughts. I quickly realized that universities operated under a different set of rules and expectations than the rest of the world. After receiving a description of my assistantship assignments by letter, I reached out to my new mentors, who I expected would be anxious for me to get started. Wrong! I emailed one of them five times before receiving any response. The other put me off until classes started. It was summertime, but many tenured academics don't work during the summer, a fact I didn't know then. (I later discovered that during the rest of the year few of them worked more than six-hour days, many were rarely seen in the office, and Fridays were the equivalent of a national holiday.) My first indoctrination to academic life revealed that some of my professors were not on speaking terms with several of their colleagues. As a student, I was bothered, but as a prospective academic I was intrigued. My education about academic life had begun.

For almost four years, I ate while standing, alternating between discount Panda Express Chinese food and partially frozen or lip-scorching Hot Pockets. I split my time between studying, writing, and doing as much remote consulting as I could to make ends meet and financially support two households. The divorce took almost two years. Six months after I left, Toni changed her mind, but I declined her offer to move to Las Vegas. I had developed a great social life: I was hanging out with my grad school buddies just like I had with the Riverview gang. Instead of weed, we had discount cocktails, and instead of my ground-floor New Jersey apartment, we hung out in casinos with cocktail waitresses. I also met a wonderful lady. Ten years later, in the darkest hour of my existence, she would keep me alive. After a few months away, I realized that I had been foolish to put off dissolving a marriage that had died by *Dieffenbachia* twenty years ago.

At UNLV, I learned valuable lessons that reinforced how little I really knew. My naïveté about academia was huge. I had no idea that I was in a top-twenty degree program as designated by *U.S. News & World Report*, or that I was being taught by some of the leading scholars in the world. Gregg Schraw, a professor and my de facto boss, took me under his wing and taught me how to write, despite my poorly calibrated sense (p. 82) of my existing writing skills. Even though I had authored more than twenty-five business publications, I was a novice at academic writing. I was now immersed in a culture of academic complication, and I needed to learn how to write to please the self-aggrandizing academic reviewers who would evaluate my research for publication in scientific journals. When academics discussed seemingly basic principles, like theories of motivation and learning, they morphed somehow into complex, elaborate philosophies with uncertain applications. Maybe "PhD" really did stand for "piled high and deep." But my goals didn't change. I made a commitment to graduate, although

Graduation day, May 2006

50 percent of my grad school peers would drop out before earning a degree. I finished in less than three and a half years, won two UNLV research awards, taught six classes as a student, presented papers at the top research conferences in my field, and was ready to move on.

Now all I needed was a job. I landed an interview with the University of Central Florida (UCF), the country's second-largest university based on student population. It was the brass ring: a tenure-track job. If, after six years of hard labor, I had met the requirements for research, teaching, and service, I would have a job indefinitely in Orlando, the happiest place on Earth—a tourist destination where everyone wanted to go. Having interviewed and hired hundreds of executives, I knew that usually the best-prepared candidate landed the job. I studied the university's history and mission, researched the backgrounds of my prospective interviewers, and mapped the routes around campus. I was ready for any questions that might arise during the mandatory presentation designed to showcase my knowledge and teaching style. I was energized and motivated, visualizing my success (p. 180) during the upcoming interview. I wanted the UCF job.

Game Changer 13: *Hoodwinked*

Too bad UCF treated me more like an unwelcome relative rather than an anticipated guest. Apparently, my interview escort had taken a vow of silence before he drove me from my hotel to the campus. I asked him questions about his research, but he only grunted; maybe he was forced into his transport role. We parked at the university, and before I could even get out of the car, I watched him scurry away; he kept an easy ten-foot lead on me all the way to the building.

   That silent, uncomfortable ride to campus turned out to be the best part of the interview. Few people attended my forty-five-minute presentation, and only one person asked a question. Maybe I bombed—maybe I didn't make any sense; I feared I was so bad they didn't want to waste their breath on a candidate they had already mentally rejected. At the obligatory candidate dinner later that night, my potential boss and her longtime colleague drank several martinis before I arrived and spent a good part of the evening talking about the dead bodies and decapitated heads they had seen on a recent trip to an academic conference in Thailand. My morning driver attended too, remaining completely silent throughout dinner. I was confused. I departed UCF not knowing whether I had dazzled or depressed my potential coworkers. I was shocked to receive an offer letter a few days later, and quick yeses to all my salary negotiation requests. It was too good to be true. Although I was somewhat

hesitant about my decision (p. 140) because of the strange interview, I accepted, ordered my Mickey Mouse ears, and started to
pack for what would turn out to be the academic equivalent of an
amusement park ride. The game had changed again.

I transitioned to academia for financial security and time control,
but a third, even more powerful, motive would ultimately influence
my happiness: the value I placed on teaching. I believed that students would want to learn from my experience working at more
than fifty companies and studying under some of the finest scholars in the world. I thought they would appreciate my knowledge
and experience and would learn from the many mistakes I had
made. And based on my UNLV experiences, I thought I would have
support from colleagues in this project. I was book-smart, but still
quite naïve.

What I found as a faculty member at UCF was worse than my
wildest fears. The academic culture I sought to embrace was mired
in favoritism. Administrators and staff made decisions based on
relationships at the expense of logic and reason. Personal gain was
paramount. I had expected organizational politics—every organization has them—but I never imagined that student learning would be
sacrificed for self-preservation. People seemed to ignore obvious
problems. My personal motivation—my desire to enhance students'
lives—seemed to be an afterthought for many of my peers, especially if helping students meant taking an unpopular stand or asking
a pointed question. While most faculty did have sincere intentions,
some didn't realize that handing out unearned A's and graduating
students who lacked competency was a disservice to the students.
Many departmental decisions were reactive, made only to avoid
the wrath of higher-ups. My colleagues seemed detached and with-
drawn, often working behind closed doors. The comradery I had experienced during most of my career, at the companies I worked at and
at UNLV, seemed nonexistent at UCF, and I didn't understand why.

As the years progressed, I figured it out. First, I learned that
academia also had a positive, satisfying, and personally rewarding
side. I and many of my dedicated faculty colleagues earned personal prosperity through hard work and sustained effort. Academia

challenged the limit of my capabilities more than any other position in my career. And the tenure process teaches resilience and humility. The bane of every tenure-earning professor is getting research published, because you only earn job security through many high-quality publications, and it may take two years or more to publish a single study. I was fortunate, though: I co-authored several publications with my mentor, Dr. Schraw. His support taught me how to publish single-author work in the top journals in my field. The publications added up, my internal reviews were outstanding in every category for eight straight years, and I realized the goal of controlling my own time. I was named to editorial boards, presented my research at the top conferences in the world, and my work earned international recognition. In May of 2012, I earned tenure and promotion with ease.

My second revelation was much darker and more disturbing. The longer I stayed, the more I grasped the hypocrisy of academia. Most students were only concerned about getting a degree. Education was just a stepping stone for their careers, and many didn't care about actual mastery. The university also appeared to have other priorities besides student learning. Glossy brochures and newspaper articles bragged about unparalleled growth, but neglected to mention that many class sizes doubled over a period of eight years. Graduation rates were trumpeted, but the 20 percent inflation of grade point averages since the 1990s was never discussed. Promotional materials emphasized the quality of learning and faculty expertise, but didn't mention that the university employed five times more staff and administrators than faculty. Faculty quality was touted, yet many units employed more temporary adjunct instructors than full-time faculty. (Many adjuncts are good teachers, of course, but many of them haven't published in years and don't know the latest research in their own fields.) Worst of all, I watched some of my colleagues fall into complacency (p. 120). They sat back and watched, complaining only in private or not at all, accepting hypocrisy to protect their jobs (p. 108). It took me ten years, but I finally figured it out: tenure is not designed to inspire creativity or promote academic freedom. Tenure is a safety net created to protect the *university*—it keeps faculty compliant and quiet.

This story might have ended badly, but I was lucky: two events shook me out of any complacency. First, on September 1, 2012, I almost died. While riding my bicycle, I was T-boned by a car running a traffic light at thirty-five miles an hour. I suffered nine broken bones. I spent seventeen days in the hospital and three months in a wheelchair. But my students would have never known; I didn't miss a day of work. Karen, the woman who I had met in Las Vegas, kept me alive, watching over me like a guardian angel. She typed my verbal responses to my online learners until I was strong enough to move my broken body to a chair and type on my own. The accident helped me realize that I wasn't built to sit back and collect disability, to take advantage of my situation and my employer. I used the accident as an opportunity for personal growth (p. 154) and demonstrated that I could succeed under any circumstances.

Second, I had plenty of time to think while I withdrew from OxyContin. I thought about my destiny while I festered in constant pain, dripping sweat during the long sleepless nights of withdrawals. I wasn't guaranteed to recover, and my thoughts were suicidal. Constant communication with one of my students gave me the strength and desire to move forward, or I might have given in and given up. Instead I had an idea—a familiar idea, the same idea that brought me to Florida in the first place. I would use my pain and my experience to help others prosper. On one of those sleepless nights, I decided I would write a book about motivation and performance. A few months later I embarked on a two-year journey, writing at least three hours every single day for five hundred days straight to produce the single-authored, 435-page textbook I described on page one of this book. That book went from conception to completion in about sixteen months. I wrote the whole thing while working a full-time job and having multiple surgeries. It took me almost four years to fully regain my strength. During that time, I spent a lot of time reflecting on what I had accomplished, and even more time ruminating on what I still needed to do. Could I compromise my beliefs by silently working in a system that I knew needed to change? No.

I had tolerated enough of the hypocrisy. It was time to change the game *one last time*. So I wrote *this* book.

Next steps

The rest of this story is about helping you be more successful. I have filtered through the most relevant scientific evidence from the fields of psychology, education, neuroscience, business, and athletics and transformed that knowledge into workable strategies that I call *Hacks*. Hacks are simple ways that people can improve their lives by becoming more efficient, more profitable, and more aware of their self-perceptions. Hacks are also the strategies and skills needed to act on our dreams and to understand why we are doing what we do. My story was designed to show you how motivational awareness, belief development, and Hack use work over the course of a lifetime, so that you can begin to analyze who you are—to understand your game changers and what prompted the important decisions in your life.

There are still some missing pieces. If you followed the links in my story, you probably realize I have already revealed many of the Hacks. Now I offer you a choice. Go back and read my story again, this time clicking on all the links. See if you can identify and determine when and how I used the Hacks. Try and figure how and why my motivational beliefs developed and what was driving my behavior. Consider what I was thinking when I made those game changing decisions. Figure out why some of the events I described had little or no bearing on who I am today. Find the strategies I used to move forward and the ones that helped me manage my emotions and gain greater personal awareness. Or forget my silly story and find *your* path. As you read on, think about when and how the motivational Hacks can help you understand your own life, the values you have constructed, and how you might change your game—on your terms and to your advantage.

CHAPTER TWO

Myths and Misconceptions

mlorenz/Shutterstock

WHEN I ASK PEOPLE to explain the difference between *knowledge* and *beliefs*, I usually receive a confused stare—like the head tilt a puzzled dog gives. There is, however, a huge difference between the two concepts. *Knowledge* is information that can be tested and proved false by scientific inquiry; it includes observations that can be replicated across different people in similar contexts. *Beliefs* are personal understandings and ways of thinking that develop out of experience. Many, but not all, beliefs are based on phenomena that can't be confirmed or disproved with science. For example, most people agree (and scientific evidence confirms) that life has both a beginning (birth) and an end (death). This is *knowledge*. Yet 61 percent of Americans *believe* in the undead—vampires, zombies, and other creatures who are sort of alive and sort of dead—although there is not any evidence to support that belief. Herein lies the problem: people routinely embrace fiction as fact, and this tendency is especially troublesome when it comes to motivational beliefs about the self and others.

Most people only know what they are taught. When was the last time you were directly taught anything about motivation science? Probably never (unless you are one of my students). You likely learned what you know about motivation and strategies from trial-and-error experience, from media reports, or from motivational messages put out by so-called "experts." But the media often misinterprets research findings to communicate the message they want you to hear, and the self-appointed gurus wrongly think they can motivate you because they themselves are motivated (and because they are charming, persuasive, and charismatic). We call these types of anecdotal evidence "common sense" or "folk wisdom," but the evidence is often wrong.

Considering how common false beliefs about motivation are, it is likely that you hold beliefs and opinions about yourself and others that are not backed by sound evidence. For example, do you believe that putting things off until the last minute helps increase productivity and efficiency because you leave yourself no time to waste? Have you ever worked hard over a long period without breaks in order to meet a deadline? Do you deliberately avoid writing things down because you have a good memory and you think recording things would be a waste of time? If you answered "yes" to any of the previous three statements, you have some misconceptions about motivation. Many of us believe anecdotes about motivation that have been scientifically falsified. Your approaches to motivational challenges may be based on flawed premises, or you may be using strategies that empirically do not work.

In this chapter, I identify the most common motivational myths and misconceptions. To win the game of life, you must know the rules for success. If your rules are based on experience rather than knowledge or your strategies are unsupported by evidence, you might deceive yourself and the people around you. So read on to dispel the Top Ten Motivation Myths and Misconceptions, and after the fairy tales are debunked, take the first step toward applying the Hacks and moving toward your goals.

Myth 1: *Some people are unmotivated.*

Reality: *Individual differences influence motivated behavior.*

Have you ever heard someone blurt out "I am just not that motivated" or "I'm just not that type of person" or "I'm afraid to try something new"? Of course you have! Everybody feels unmotivated sometimes: maybe we are reluctant to meet new people, or we feel lethargic, or we hate the idea of leaving the house and being forced to be sociable. Sometimes we internalize this lack of motivation and think there's something wrong with us. In other words, we develop motivational *perceptions*, sometimes unconsciously, about ourselves and others. At other times, we externalize our lack of motivation, aiming our anger at the systems we feel keep us from succeeding: for example, students tell me, "Classes are boring," "I hate my job," or "Education is pointless if I can't get a good job." As the second group of statements show, we always seek to find justified reasons and causes for our actions.

What do I mean by "perception" here? Perceptions are the things we believe about ourselves; they influence our behaviors, including what challenges we accept and how likely we are to successfully complete tasks. For example, if you doubt your mathematics ability—if you have a negative perception of how good you are at math—you're not likely to consider a career as an actuary. We internalize harsh criticism from others and our own self-doubt, and these internalized perceptions can create disengagement and apathy. But your self-perceptions may or may not be accurate; they are determined by how you evaluate yourself and how you interpret your own behavior. Warped perceptions can cascade into mistaken generalizations about your ability and your effort. Thus, before we dig into the Hacks, let's make sure you're not going to use them on the wrong thing, or in the wrong way. Let's first evaluate the myths and misconceptions we hold about ourselves.

The most common misconception is the belief that people are either motivated or unmotivated. When we observe behavior that differs from our own, we tend to incorrectly guess the causes of that behavior. This is because humans have an innate curiosity about why things happen. Like two-year-olds (who ask "why" every thirty seconds), adults wonder why people do what they do. When people behave differently from us and we disapprove of that behavior (maybe it conflicts with our own experience and beliefs), we infer that the person is unmotivated. Think of the spouse, sibling, friend, or child in their pajamas all day, watching TV while you head to work at seven o'clock a.m. We might read this behavior as meaning the person is unmotivated; what it really means is the person is driven by a different set of standards and beliefs than our own. When we decide someone is unmotivated, we are making a value judgment: if that person is unmotivated, we are psychologically superior, right? And feeling superior is a great way to boost our egos and jumpstart our own personal motivation. Actually, there is no such thing as being unmotivated. People are just motivated by different things, and motivation changes *all the time*.

Myth 2: *People are motivationally equal.*

Reality: *Motivation differs in direction and intensity based on context, culture, and beliefs.*

Another common misconception is the fallacy of motivational equality. Despite what the Declaration of Independence says, people are not created equal, because people in the exact same circumstances display a broad range of motivational intensity. People set obviously different goals based on diverse personal values. And even when everything else is equal, people have vast differences in commitment levels. To see motivational inequality in action, visit one of my classes and observe my students. Some students sit passively;

others participate as eagerly as Hermione Granger in Potions class at Hogwarts. They are all generally equal in academic ability, and they all have the same final goal—to earn a good enough grade to graduate. But that shared goal catalyzes a wide range of behaviors. Some submit no homework, or the bare minimum; others ask for extra work. And someone who submits homework doesn't necessarily care about learning. I didn't go to college because I cared about learning; I went because I was afraid of Renee's wrath (p. 15). If you assume motivational equality across individuals, you are making serious judgment errors, because the same behaviors may represent a variety of motives and the same motives may produce a variety of behaviors.

A perfect example of the differences between thinking and behavior can be seen in a classic psychology study. The day after Dr. Martin Luther King Jr. was assassinated, a third-grade teacher named Jane Elliott wanted to show her students what it was like to be judged differently because of their skin color. Jane told her students that children with blue eyes were superior to children with brown eyes. She gave the blue-eyed children extra privileges, like longer recess and more food during snack time, and denied the brown-eyed kids the same privileges. She made the brown-eyed kids wear pilgrim collars so they could be easily identified as belonging to the brown-eyed group even at a distance. By the time her experiment in prejudice ended, the blue-eyed children were openly vicious, aggressive, and arrogant toward the brown-eyed children. Jane had manipulated the blue-eyed students into believing they were superior. Jane repeated the experiment, this time reversing the roles and giving preference to the brown-eyed children. The same thing happened. In both cases, the feeling of superiority changed students' normal classroom behavior. When it comes to motivation, many of us think like those children with their artificially induced feelings of power. Jane Elliott's experiment lays bare how fleeting and unstable motives are.

Although Jane Elliot's experiment was contrived, motivational inequality has plenty of practical implications. If you go outside in the pouring rain and get uncomfortably wet, you'll probably change your behavior next time it rains; you'll either take an umbrella or stay in the house until the rain stops. If you don't mind getting wet—and some people love to dance in the rain—you'll venture out regardless; your behavior won't change. This example shows that your getting-wet beliefs and your reactions to precipitation influence your actions: we repeat behaviors that work for us. But everyone else in the world doesn't have the same perceptions of rain and reality as you do, and this difference creates motivational disparities. If your experience is rewarding, satisfying, or even just good enough, you will believe that your way of operating is appropriate. The diversity of experience breeds motivational differences, and these differences come into play as you make and defend your life choices.

Myth 3: *You are a motivational type.*

Reality: *There are types of motivation, but no motivational types.*

Labeling is a huge problem for understanding motivation. Labeling lumps common characteristics together, speeds assessment time, and supposedly simplifies the understanding of branded individuals, but labels are purely for convenience. They make it easier to conceptualize, justify, and predict the behavior of others, but aren't actually all that accurate. The categorization process often results in misclassifications. We label *everything*, down to demographic basics like calling people "boys" and "girls." But do all boys act the same way? No! Do all girls act the same way? No! Stereotypes, which ascribe similar traits to all individuals in certain categories, are nothing but labels gone wrong. Labeling is equally useless when it comes to motivation. Although there is plenty of scientific evidence that there are different types of motivation, there is none to indicate that people have a fixed motivational *type*. Believing in motivational types is nothing more than stereotyping behavior rather than physical characteristics.

But business and the media make tons of money by labeling and categorizing people. *Answer a few simple questions to discover your personality or your motivational type! Are you the romantic type or are you the leadership type?* According to a recent BuzzFeed quiz, I am a peanut butter cookie type. Labeling people as belonging to different motivational types is as silly (and about as scientifically accurate) as that BuzzFeed quiz. The process is inaccurate and is likely to lead to false conclusions. Motives change all the time, and there is no such thing as a motivational type.

Think about your own behavior and emotions: you are not the same every day. You likely feel and act differently about different tasks on different days. Pick any goal, desired outcome, or job, and evaluate your degree of invested effort. Your intensity changed from day to day, right? Effort investments fluctuate. Why would a label that doesn't apply probably 90 percent of the time be useful? Of course, we have dominant traits and familiar behavior patterns that help us navigate the world, but we don't conform to fixed patterns of behavior. Think you are a visual learner? Let me know how you learn visually when listening to music! You are just a learner. If your perceptions of yourself or others are based on stable traits like ethnicity, religion, IQ, learning styles—anything people can't change about themselves—you are making judgment errors. Labels give us a false image or vision of the person, and the labeled person begins to think they should act like the stereotype or the label. This is treacherous territory; these false beliefs may limit or enhance people's ability to accomplish things. Labels belong on jars, not people.

●

Myth 4: *You are the best judge of your own motives.*

Reality: *Self-views are clouded by other people, thinking biases, and cultural norms.*

Many people believe they are the best judges of their own motives—after all, who knows you better than you know yourself? But there is a problem with the information that we use during self-evaluation. It is evidence from personal experience, which is colored by deeply held world views. In other words, objectivity is a problem for self-evaluation. Our perspectives are always encumbered by emotions, customs, and thinking biases that are almost impossible to suspend. Yet we often rely on our own idiosyncratic perspectives to understand ourselves and the people around us.

For example, I was bitten three times by dogs as a child. Because of this, I avoid parks, kennels, hot dogs, and Beethoven movies, because I am uncomfortable around canines. Dogs are unpredictable, and my avoidance is justified based on my experience. Are my canine perceptions defensible and accurate? Not really. The problem is not dogs, but what I think and expect when I encounter a dog, based on my past experiences. My dog thoughts and perceptions are completely biased, and I interpret them based on my unique set of behavior patterns and my experiences with the world. No matter how hard you try to persuade me that my dog beliefs are flawed and that your dog is darling, I will continue to avoid dogs, because I believe that is the best way to navigate my life. It's nearly impossible for us to objectively identify our own motives and the emotions that go along with those motives, and those motives and emotions can cloud our judgment and confound our behavior.

Let's talk about another psychological experiment. Unlike Jane Elliott's, this one isn't famous; it's one that I conduct with my classes. I separate students into two groups and ask them to read the same three-paragraph story about a house. The paragraphs describe the location, occupants, design, interior features, and landscape of the house. I tell the students that they have three minutes to read the three hundred words and to remember as many details as they can. At the end of the three minutes, they write down the things they remember most from the story—the most salient details— without looking at the story again and discuss what they thought were the five most important details with their peers. There is a difference in the instructions I give the two student groups, though: the first group is told to pretend they are real estate agents as they read the story, and the second group is told to read the story from the perspective of a criminal. The two groups recall two completely different sets of facts, each highly influenced by the imagined career perspectives. This is selective recall—meaning that what we see, remember, and consider important is rooted in our own biased perspectives—and it is practically unavoidable.

Personal preference also clouds self-analysis. If we went out to lunch together, I might order a bowl of lukewarm succotash (lima beans and corn). You might be grossed out, preferring a cheese-burger and fries. We make our decisions based on what we believe is best, and opinion often drives our decision-making. Even if there were a "best" menu choice, a lifetime of experience dictates what we order—some of us decide based on taste, some based on price, some based on particular foods' emotional associations, and some based on nutritional profile. We are all opinionated and we all believe that our way is the best way. Keith Stanovich, a favorite author of mine, calls this "myside bias"—basically, this cognitive bias says "my way or the highway." Ultimately, we can assess our own motives about as well as we can determine the color of the sky while wearing six pairs of sunglasses. We may think our impressions are accurate, but our vision is obscured, and our conclusions are likely wrong.

•

Myth 5: *People believe the truth.*

Reality: *We seek and filter evidence to support our personal beliefs.*

Personal preference and individual experience cascade into a second type of flawed thinking called *confirmation bias*. This type of misconception occurs because we look for evidence to support our beliefs, but ignore or reject evidence that might disconfirm them. In practice, overlooking evidence influences behavior. For example, rabid football fans might downplay the drama of a nail-biting baseball game; it doesn't matter to them that any single pitch can influence the outcome of the entire game, or that the difference between winning and losing is often one player's performance. If we believe that football is better than baseball, we will have a long list of reasons that defend our football preference. Most people believe that everyone is entitled to their own opinion, even if it's wrong.

Confirmation bias brings us back to the distinction between knowledge and beliefs from the introduction to this chapter. By now you may have realized that self-beliefs influence motivation more than anything else. When we back up what we believe with *empirical* evidence—evidence gathered using the scientific method—we are relying on knowledge. This type of evidence is collected under systematic, controlled conditions in order to test a hypothesis about the world; replicating the conditions under which it was gathered produces similar outcomes. For example, rain is the same in North America and in South America: in both places, people get wet, crops get watered, puddles develop. There aren't many different interpretations of precipitation evidence, because that evidence is replicated across people and across situations. But what if you *believe* that, when you go outside in the rain, the raindrops burn red scars into your face? When we lean on belief to back up our opinions, we are using personal experience instead of evidence, and personal experience cannot be replicated. Just as a fingerprint is a unique biological marker, so is your psychological experience: it is only known to you. If I go outside in the same rain and I get no red scars, then (no matter how hard you believe it) your belief is unsupported and flawed—repeating the experiment did not produce the same results. These are two different ways of looking at the physical world, evidence, and opinion.

Our beliefs about ourselves and our internal worlds can rarely be replicated and confirmed by others. If you think that going out in the rain will scar your face, that belief—even though it cannot be substantiated by others—influences your behavior. Unless you want a scarred complexion, you will stay inside when it rains. People simply believe things that are not true. And when those false beliefs are about our own competence and capabilities, things get messy. If you believe you can never be confident and successful when meeting new people, your belief will generate anxiety, and you will probably avoid parties and networking opportunities to insulate yourself from discomfort and embarrassment. (And don't worry, Hacks can help you solve the social avoidance problem; p. 198).

Myth 6: *Determining reasons for behavior and events is simple.*

Reality: *There are multiple causes, including culture and development, for human behavior.*

Conventional wisdom says that being out in bad weather, or feeling cold, makes you more likely to catch a cold. These beliefs, which keep many people snuggled indoors during the cold winter months, developed because we want to explain why things happen in simplistic and understandable terms. Cultural norms and habitual behavior patterns encourage this kind of naïve thinking about causation. But little (if any) scientific evidence supports the notion that weather contributes to getting sick. Ironically, the *real* reason more people get sick during the winter is that they spend more time inside with other people, cozily sealed up inside petri-dish buildings, rubbing elbows with potential cold carriers. But scientific fact doesn't help dispel people's false beliefs. My mother still told me, "Wear a sweater or you'll catch a cold." You can't argue with your mom, but sweater beliefs, like other falsehoods, are passed on because they are intuitive explanations of common phenomena.

Other false beliefs are passed on because of tradition. I once heard a story about how a mother and her two daughters prepared holiday celebration meals. Every year before Thanksgiving and Christmas, the two daughters watched their mother cut the ends off the turkey before cooking it and throw the ends in the garbage. The daughters grew older and had families of their own. When they cooked their own turkey dinners, they also cut off the ends of the turkey and threw them in the trash. One year, the mother asked the older daughter why she did this. The daughter said, "It was what you always did, so I thought I should do it too." The mother said, "I only cut the ends off the turkey because the whole bird wouldn't fit in our little oven."

The turkey example reveals how much personal values and cultural customs influence behavior. Tradition is highly resistant to change, even when it goes against logic and reason. Misconceptions persist in individuals, families, and organizations because we tend to repeat the behaviors that we observe. But traditions often have no objective basis in scientific fact. The daughters believed that trimming the turkey was part of the correct turkey-cooking method, and they did what they saw as normal without questioning why.

Many false beliefs are based on false causality—the idea that some particular event, person, or phenomenon is directly responsible for an observed outcome. This mistake happens when you confuse correlation and causality—when you don't consider that a third, less obvious, factor may be driving the behavior you observed. The popular media is especially guilty of this. How many times have you heard that video games cause aggressive behavior, or that paying people more always improves their performance? Both of these claims conflict with scientific evidence, but we tend to assume that outcomes have a single cause, so these false claims resonate with us and we believe them. Remember two-year-olds with their incessant "why" questions? ("I'm not cold. Why do I have to wear a sweater when I go outside?" "I miss Mommy. Why do I have to go to school?" Why is Daddy so happy on Sunday mornings?") Adults subconsciously ask the same "why" questions; we are always searching for the causes of observed events. After all, we learned early that one thing leads to another. A baby who pushes the bowl of squash puree off her highchair tray learns that gravity works, that squash splatters, and that she doesn't have to eat food that has hit the floor. But as adults, we (wrongly) apply this simple causative physical logic to other, more complex events.

Later we explore the *Integration Hack* (p. 77), which explains that most things have multiple synergistic causes. In the section explaining the *Integration Hack*, I use the example of a job interview that doesn't result in an offer. You might want to blame one single cause for the rejection: maybe you misspoke, maybe your values were different from the recruiter's, or maybe you forgot the pre-interview Listerine. We can usually only speculate. Ultimately, the only thing you can *know* is that another candidate was better suited for the opportunity, but we rarely see things that way. Instead, we look for causes and make interpretation mistakes.

People take advantage of the causative fallacy, using it to support their beliefs by attributing causality to things that are only

correlated. My colleague and videographer, Dr. Feenstra, who helped with the book, created a great video that shows a very strong positive relationship between the amount of ice cream people eat and the murder rate. Does ice cream agitate people and make them more aggressive?

YouTube video:
Ice Cream–Murder

Does the increase in ice cream sales *cause* the rise in murder rates? (Honestly, I think *not* eating ice cream would make people more anxious and cranky and likely to lose it.) Yes, there is a positive relationship between ice cream and murder, but neither one causes the other. In fact, *hot weather* causes both increases. People eat more ice cream when it's hot. They also commit more murders when it's hot; not only are they outside their houses, mixing with people who might piss them off, but they are also physically uncomfortable and on edge. It's very easy to assume causality where there is only correlation, and uninformed people apply this logic in their own lives, basing decisions on false conclusions that are not grounded in factual evidence.

Myth 7: *Other people can motivate you.*

Reality: *Personal beliefs and appropriate strategy use lead to optimal performance.*

This is a myth that is perpetuated in the psychological self-help community: some people claim to be naturally able to motivate others. Their confidence, although genuine, is usually based on idiosyncratic theories of motivation that worked in their own lives but that can't be tested. Just because someone has enough charisma to convince you that their approach transformed their life, it doesn't mean the strategy will also work for you. Beware of impersonators who claim that their method guarantees results (and run from those who use terms like *always*, *never*, or *everyone*; rarely is anything that absolute)! Their theories of motivation are usually untested and unsupported by evidence.

Theories are interpretations of phenomena that structure our understanding of people, events, and behavior. But not all theories are created equal. For example, I have a theory that eating bacon makes you happier than having baconaphobia. Can you debunk my theory? Probably not, because happiness is subjective—my theory of well-being through bacon can't be tested. The ironic thing about theories is that only the good ones can be falsified. Good theories work until they don't any more. In other words, theories stick around until disconfirming evidence is discovered. My bacon theory is impossible to refute because it's my opinion. We develop these kinds of untestable personal theories as we go through life collecting evidence and information and forming impressions about people, phenomena, and our experiences. For some people, life really is all about the bacon.

When people continue to embrace personal theories even in the face of disconfirming evidence, the theory turns into a false belief—in psychology, we call it "pseudoscience." Examples include believing in palm reading, tarot cards, Ouija boards, Punxsutawney Phil (the weather-predicting groundhog), and bad luck on Friday the 13th—as well as certain views about motivation. All these theories are flawed, both because the results cannot be replicated across different people and contexts and because they *cannot be falsified*. And when these theories don't work, the person who benefits from perpetuating the false belief usually says it was your fault: you are a nonbeliever, you lack understanding, or you did something wrong. In other words, when evidence refutes a belief and personal benefit becomes the only reason to continue supporting it, it's time to junk that belief. (By the way, did I mention that donations to the Hack Your Motivation team vacation fund increase intelligence, self-esteem, and youthful appearance? Believe me!)

The charismatic, misguided motivational hucksters are trying to convince you to give up control and adopt their beliefs. The motivators want you to think like them, to believe they can inspire you. It's true that good role models can give a little nudge to your behavior and can accelerate skill development, but that's all they can do. These professional motivators only succeed when their followers hang on to naïve misconceptions about motivation. Remember that motives change all the time, based on your task or goal, your personal development, your context, and your culture. To believe someone can magically motivate you by their own behavior contradicts just about every scientific principle of motivation. How could anyone know your personal beliefs and what motivates you in a particular situation? It is as unlikely that a generic, universally effective motivational strategy will ever work in practice as it is that a mythical Pennsylvania groundhog can accurately and consistently predict the weather.

What the self-proclaimed motivational gurus *don't* do is provide followers with evidence-based strategies that promote life success. If they offered effective strategies instead of personal testimonials, they would be putting themselves out of business. Instead, the gurus often capitalize on the insecurity of people who believe they can't change in the direction of happiness by themselves. These impressionable people don't know that intense motivation is rooted in self-confidence and can be nurtured with strategies that help them reach their goals. Ultimately, the most successful people are those who retain motivational control (p. 209), believing that they can attain their goals on their own. There is a substantial difference between learning how to use the research-based strategies I call "Hacks" and adopting personal recommendations from gurus. *Hack Your Motivation* is very different from the advice offered by Tony Robbins, Tamara Lowe, and countless others professing to sell motivational insight that, when followed to the letter, will transform your life. What these people are really selling is nothing more than the anxiety reduction that comes from surrendering control to others.

Myth 8: *Heredity does not influence motivation.*

Reality: *Most aspects of human development have some heritable basis.*

Research shows that people need nurturing and environmental support to reach their potential. So why do people say there are "born" leaders, teachers, or athletes? As these two views of motivation suggest, success is influenced by *both* environment (nurture) and biology (nature). If we believe that Marcus Jordan's skill at basketball is purely genetic, we ignore the effect of years of practice and feedback from his father Michael Jordan, one of the best basketball players in history.

Heredity clearly matters for physical attributes and athletic per-formance, and it also influences motivation to perform and excel. In my motivation courses, I ask my students on the first day of class, "How many of you think your motivation is governed by heredity and genetics? If your parents are crabby, does that mean you're likely to be crabby? If your ancestors were creative, entrepreneur-ial, friendly, or aggressive, does that have any influence on you?" Invariably, 60 percent of students don't believe genetics influence their motivation (dispositions, emotions, and effort tendencies). In fact, motivational qualities are no different than physical traits: roughly 50 percent of your motivational tendencies are determined by heredity, and the other 50 percent are shaped by your environ-ment. Your environment will encourage some inherited motivational attributes and suppress others; even those who are born docile and quiet can learn, with guidance and support, to become as atten-tion-getting as Ozzy Osbourne (although maybe without biting the heads off bats).

For example, if you were encouraged as a child to read all the time, you are more likely to be studious than if you were constantly encouraged to play aggressive contact sports. Parents can either nurture or ignore an inborn trait. Simply having a certain genetic tendency doesn't mean that trait will dominate your behavior. The reality is that upbringing often overrides genetic traits, provided we have opportunities to perform and excel (which are not guaranteed). Without a fighting chance to develop (a chance that people born into oppression and poverty don't have), strong inborn motivational qualities cannot reach their full potential.

●

Myth 9: *Sustained superhuman motivation is a fantasy.*

Reality: *Conditions related to peak performance are personal and possible.*

Is it possible to achieve a state of consistent peak performance, where everything seems to go right and we easily achieve our desired outcomes? This optimal motivation state requires ideal contextual and motivational conditions: a sufficiently challenging task that you have the skills or knowledge to complete, physical health (a well-rested and well-nourished body), a mind and performance environment free of cognitive and emotional intrusions, and motivation to persevere in the face of obstacles. While it's rare to hit all these ideal conditions at once, you can achieve optimal motivation when you master a variety of strategies and have the motivation to use your talents. The most important takeaway here is that peak performance strategies are learned.

For optimal motivation, you have to believe that you can control and orchestrate successful outcomes. If you don't believe you have the tools needed to succeed, it's unlikely that you'll exert the effort needed to achieve excellence. Giving up your sense of control always dilutes optimal performance; this is what happens when you surrender your power to fake motivational gurus (p. 90). In other words, we must believe that we can reach our desired outcomes in order to perform at our peak. Control beliefs—our expectation that we can get what we want—are a key determinant of performance. People with elevated control beliefs use more productive strategies than people with low control beliefs. But even if you don't currently have the ideal combination of ability, beliefs, and strategies, the Hacks are designed to propel you forward and help you capitalize on your potential. Motivational superiority, like most other skills, requires dedicated practice and targeted feedback. Knowing the Hacks can often be the competitive edge that moves you from mediocre outcomes to optimal results. Never doubt your abilities, or you may fail no matter how talented you are.

Myth 10: *Behavior signifies motive.*

Reality: *The same behavior can represent different or multiple motives.*

A few years back, Karen and I took a day-trip to Tangier, Morocco—a majority-Muslim city in northern Africa where most residents have ultra-conservative religious and cultural values—especially during the sacred celebration of Ramadan. Our hired guide, Omar, met us at the pier upon our arrival by hydrofoil from Spain, and we walked around Tangier for about eight hours. We wanted to see as much as possible, so (using my optimal tourism strategy) I walked relatively fast—not much faster than I would walk back home in the United States, though. Omar, who was walking slowly and talking to Karen, shouted after me, "Why are you walking so fast, Bob?" I responded, "What do you mean, Omar? This is how I walk all the time." Omar answered, "When you walk that fast in Morocco, people think that you have stolen something. You must walk more slowly here." Having been raised in the hustle and bustle of New York City, I hadn't realized that my normal pace was inappropriate in this context and might be misinterpreted. The moral of the story is that behavior does not accurately represent motives.

Perhaps you are not traveling to Tangier this week and would prefer a more mundane example. On the first day of class, I ask students, "Why are you taking this class?" The question is designed to see if students can detect their own motives. Some students say, "I'm taking the class because it's required" or "I'm conforming and doing what I'm supposed to." Some say, "I'm taking the class because it will help me gain more knowledge about motivation." Others say, "I'm taking this class because my parents made me go to college." Still others say, "I'm taking the class because I want to show everyone how smart I am." That's five different reasons given for the exact same class-taking behavior. Never confidently infer a single motive from behavior, because you'll very often be wrong.

●

We have discussed the most common motivational misinterpretations people embrace. Since we now know some of the many reasons why interpretation of behavior can go awry, we are on a clearer path to accurately assess our own and others' motives. But there are many more factors to consider before reaching conclusions and acting on our escalating motivational knowledge; I call these factors *Awareness Hacks*, and they are described in the next segment of the book. Until you develop a keen awareness and a strongly objective stance, it will be practically impossible for you to use the forthcoming Hacks for maximal gain.

CHAPTER THREE

Awareness Hacks

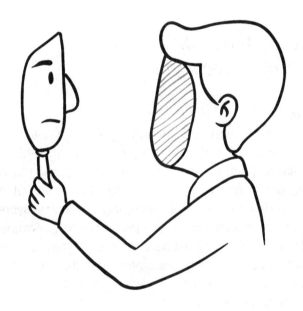

HAVING DISPELLED THE MYTHS and misconceptions about how motivation is interpreted, we now turn to problems with how behavior is analyzed. *Awareness Hacks* focus on strategies for successful behavior assessment. As you read this section, keep in mind the old saying—you don't know what you don't know. Motivational influences often operate below the level of consciousness. Humans tend to see, feel, and hear only what is obvious, sometimes jumping to conclusions without thorough investigation. *Awareness Hacks* will help you accurately identify motives and analyze behavior—in yourself and in others.

1. Wake-Up Hack—*Make the unconscious conscious.*

The details

Lack of personal awareness almost guarantees failure at work, school, and life in general, but many people avoid self-awareness. We don't like to think about unpleasant events, people we dislike, obligations, or things we would like to change about ourselves. Some people use avoidance as a coping strategy, psychologically sweeping life stressors under the proverbial rug. Avoidance insulates us from conflict and makes us feel better. Others choose repression to cope, putting uncomfortable thoughts out of their minds with excuses and justifications. Humans are wired to avoid pain and seek pleasure. Living by "out of sight, out of mind" lets us temporarily insulate ourselves from reality and avoid experiencing negative emotions. You see why we need *Awareness Hacks*!

But avoiding worrisome thoughts and ignoring reality doesn't change actual problems. You won't be able to use the *Action Hacks* (p. 153) described later in the book if you don't first recognize the need for the Hack or don't know when and how to use the Hack. The *Wake-Up Hack* asks you to invest deliberate and intentional effort to transform your habitual and unconscious thoughts and bring them into the forefront of your mind. Although making the unconscious conscious may produce temporary discomfort or anxiety, doing so allows you to address the real challenges you face. Awareness is the foundation for potential growth, so let's start by getting your thoughts up on your personal radar screen.

Why it works

Cognitive scientists generally agree that there are two types of thinking—let's call them Type 1 and Type 2 (after Dr. Seuss's Thing One and Thing Two). Type 1 thinking happens automatically, below the level of consciousness, and is guided by our personal beliefs and experience. Type 1 thinking requires minimal effort and feels intuitive. Examples of Type 1 thinking are reading the words on this page, recognizing a face, or finding your way to the bathroom in your house. Type 2 thinking is effortful and requires focused attention. This is the type of thinking used when looking for lost keys, solving a math problem, or deciding whether five dollars is too much to pay for a lottery ticket.

Behavior is often determined by which type of thinking you use. When you default to Type 1 thinking, you let intuition and habit take over. Type I thinking might mean you impulsively take a few bites of succulent chocolate cake, even though you know it is unhealthy and high in calories. To change your behavior, you must engage in Type 2 thinking. But humans typically prefer to avoid Type 2 thinking. It requires effort, and we don't like to expend effort unless we believe there will be a significant benefit. With Type 2 thinking, you would probably choose not to eat the cake, but only after thoughtful deliberation. The same process applies to personal awareness. We must consciously work to override our tendency to rely on familiar and comfortable ways of thinking; being aware, which requires Type 2 thinking, leads to more objective evaluations of your circumstances and clearer decision-making.

Application

The *Wake-Up Hack* can be used any time you might later regret a decision. The Hack should be used to honestly answer the question of *why* you are choosing to engage in an activity, or *why* you are taking a specific approach to achieve a goal. This Hack is designed to focus attention on all available evidence before acting. I surely should have used the *Wake-Up Hack* when I decided not to mail

YouTube video:
Wake Up

Dr. Yu's China package (p. 24). Simple tactics can promote clarity in thinking. Ask yourself, "What is the real reason for this action?" or "Am I considering the possible consequences of my behavior?" The *Wake-Up Hack* is especially useful when you are considering an action that might be inappropriate, unethical, or politically incorrect. Considering whether you would decide the same if others were around is one good test. Another approach is to evaluate your reasoning process as if the behavior has already been completed. If you had thought about potential negative outcomes, would you have taken the same steps? If you had a second chance, would you change your behavior? Would you have downed the extra beer at the bar if you knew there was a police officer on the next corner? Ultimately, the success of the *Wake-Up Hack* depends on considering all available evidence and potential outcomes before moving forward.

2. **Buy Later Hack**—*Practice critical thinking to avoid emotionally triggered decisions.*

The details
Closely related to the *Wake-Up Hack* is the *Buy Later Hack*. Both Hacks are designed to encourage sound evaluation of evidence to promote effective decision-making. The *Buy Later Hack* is specifically designed to avoid the impulsiveness caused by emotional, rather than logical, decision-making. Emotions fall into the automatic Type 1 thinking category; we must be intentional about changing our automatic *reaction* into a planned, rational *strategy*. Lawyers, politicians, and salespeople thrive on making emotional appeals with the hope that the automatic reaction will prompt a

quick decision in their favor. These cunning linguists specialize in emotional manipulation, triggering positive emotions with words like *honesty*, *faith*, and *intelligence*, and strategically activating unfavorable feelings about the opposition with words like *insulting*, *agitated*, and *offensive*. They do this to sway decisions, encourage spontaneous purchases, and create self-doubt.

The *Buy Later Hack* is designed to counteract emotion and impulsive reactions by inspiring rational thought. Critical thinking about a situation helps override the automatic emotional response; instead, it encourages you to objectively evaluate solutions using logic and reason. Thinking critically is not just the suppression of impulse. It requires a basic openness to different perspectives on shared problems and a willingness to leave behind snap decisions. Like the *Wake-Up Hack*, the *Buy Later Hack* requires effortful thinking; you must acknowledge that you can only choose the best course of action after deliberate thought.

Why it works

Many people have inflexible opinions that are based on deeply entrenched beliefs formed over a lifetime. These beliefs can involve anything from your favorite color to the best way to garnish a hotdog to when you should make charitable donations. We also have beliefs about problem-solving in general—about the best way to accomplish our personal goals and objectives. Some of us are intuitive and make snap decisions on limited information; others are more deliberate and intentional, weighing all options and available evidence. Spontaneous individuals will ardently defend their approach, but in reality, they often decide based on personal bias and only look for information to confirm their decision (p. 59), ignoring contrary evidence. While spontaneity is essential in a crisis, most decisions allow you time to make the best choice—one you won't later regret.

Critical thinkers are more successful at solving problems; they are more open to trying new approaches than their spontaneous peers, and they usually have concrete reasons for their choices. Critical thinkers are also more efficient at setting attainable goals and correcting mistakes (and they frequently win arguments and debates). Like other acquired skills, critical thinking is learned through effort and through practice. To improve our thinking processes, we must intentionally evaluate our thoughts and practice overriding emotionally charged decisions. When we aren't actively thinking, others take advantage of our cognitive laziness. Have you ever wondered why candy and gum are sold by the checkout counter at grocery stores? It's not for your convenience: this strategic placement is designed to separate you from your money by exploiting impulsive decision-making. This intentional selling strategy takes advantage of the limited checkout time, giving you the feeling that you must decide quickly, without time to think and reason. The good news is that critical thinking works across problems and situations. If you are conscious and aware, you can outwit even the craftiest retailers, lawyers, and salespeople by using the *Buy Later Hack.*

Application

Taking time to think is especially important during negotiations. Although many work cultures make you feel you must make a quick decision (think about my Trellis offer—I quickly agreed to his deal because I was excited [p. 32] about the inflated salary), they do this intentionally, to keep you from thinking critically about what they're offering. If I had evaluated the decision circumstances in the Trellis situation, I would have realized that his demand for an immediate decision was a red flag. Reputable companies rarely hire employees without reference checks; by not verifying my work experience, Trellis was showing me that he didn't care about my character or ethics—he wanted someone vulnerable that he could control. I made a snap decision, carried away by the salary, and discounted other highly pertinent factors that I surely should have paid attention to.

The *Buy Later Hack* can also help you make purchases or personal commitments that you will still feel good about long after the decision. Crafty salespeople, real estate agents, and especially car dealers will detect your emotional connection to a product and exploit it. The seemingly uninterested buyer who can walk away usually gets the best deal. It is cheaper and far more satisfying to get a call the next day from a salesperson who has mysteriously found a better deal for you than it is to buy at full price under the influence of emotion. The *Buy Later Hack* also helps in other highly charged, emotional situations; it might keep you safer (you won't chase after that possibly armed driver who cut you off) and it might prevent a lifetime of disappointment by helping you avoid snap decisions about relationships. You might come to regret not using the *Buy Later Hack* before saying yes to a spontaneous marriage proposal. For any decision, whether it's potentially life altering or merely an impulsive bubblegum purchase, use the *Buy Later Hack* and avoid making an emotional decision you might regret.

3. **Integration Hack**—*Avoid attributing the cause of behavior or outcome to one source.*

The details

Nearly everything in nature has a complex, not a simple, cause: it doesn't snow every time the air is cold, sunshine alone doesn't keep plants alive, and fires won't burn without fuel *and* oxygen. Similarly, the underlying motives that drive human behavior are complex and interlocking. Simplified explanations of behavior are always flawed. To accurately understand our behavior, we must realize that the actions that move us toward our goals come out of the complex interaction between our context and our personal beliefs. If you normally curse like a sailor, do you do it in front of your parents, in the library, or in church? The *Integration Hack* helps us see that neither our successes nor our failures can be attributed to one single cause.

Success comes from a combination of having the appropriate knowledge (the skill), devoting effort to the task (the will to achieve), and closely monitoring our outcomes to determine whether we are on target. Have you ever been turned down for a job after an interview? How did you react? Did you blame the rejection on a single cause (the New-Jersey-shaped spaghetti-sauce stain on your necktie, an internal candidate's edge, or the interviewer's failure to recognize your vast experience and stellar achievements)? Typically, when we succeed, we attribute that success internally, to our own worth. When we fail, we point fingers at others and attribute the failure externally. We rarely recognize that most outcomes—success or failure—come from a complex interaction of multiple factors. The *Integration Hack* teaches us that we can't understand motivation when we look at behavior in isolation.

Why it works

Humans look for causes. Remember two-year-olds and their obsession with asking why? Adults, too, look for patterns and causes to help make sense of the world. If you watch TV crime dramas, you know the prosecution looks for a motive to get a conviction. Lawyers need to explain to the jury why the criminal did what he did. But there are two problems with our incessant quest to understand the world: first, we often attribute an event to the wrong cause, and second, we usually fix on a simple solution rather than a complex one. Remember the causation myth (p. 60)? Behaviors and events might be caused, not by the seemingly simple, single cause in which you believe, but by a hidden factor. In other words, remember that murder is not caused by ice cream. It is important to know that ice cream and murder are *related*, because hot weather both increases the desire to eat cold foods and contributes to discomfort, making us more susceptible to emotional reactions. But we shouldn't oversimplify and believe in death by Popsicle.

We look for easy-to-understand solutions that don't require much effort; we are quick to jump to conclusions. For example, what is the first thing you do after a fender bender? Probably try to decide whose fault it was. Maybe we blame it on the other driver: he was distracted, or he's a terrible driver. Maybe we blame it on the environment: it was raining, or there was a pothole, or it was Friday the 13th. Most likely, multiple factors caused the accident.

Perhaps the other driver was distracted *and* didn't see the pothole until too late *and* the rain-slick roads weren't forgiving of his swerve.

Our understanding of what causes things to happen is further complicated by the fact that we are prone to *thinking fallacies*—judgment errors that we fall into when evaluating physical and psychological phenomena. These errors include inappropriate generalization (all dogs are vicious), falling prey to the either/or conundrum (people are good or evil, but not both), thinking there are no alternative explanations (an unexplained noise is definitely a ghost), and, of course, coincidence (the outcome was the result of pure chance, beyond any human intervention or control). Between thinking fallacies and our preference for obvious, simple explanations, we struggle to understand our own motives and behaviors.

Application

The *Integration Hack* can help you think about the multiple causes of an event, motive, or behavior. It's systemic thinking. In the workplace, for example, when successes and failures are analyzed, it's rarely found that one person caused a particular outcome. Organizational success is achieved through a combination of commitment, engagement, clear objectives and expectations, and leaders who support employees. Similarly, students' academic success and failure aren't the sole responsibility of the professor. Academic outcomes are also affected by the design of instructional materials, by the learner's educational history, and by how engaged the learner is, among other factors. And in relationships, one party is never solely responsible for how good the relationship is or how long it lasts; relationship outcomes grow out of compatibility and effective partnerships.

YouTube video:
Integration

The *Integration Hack* is most useful when applied to understanding the self. It is always easier to shift blame or give credit to a single external source, but self-analysis requires us to suspend our biases and systematically explore how particular outcomes were achieved. One strategy is to write down a step-by-step list of the assumptions made that contributed to an outcome. For example, if you get lost on a road trip, it's never *only* because you don't know the area. It might also be because you didn't prepare in advance (buying a map, printing out directions), because you didn't want to ask for directions, because you spaced out while driving and missed your exit, or because you hate to admit you screwed up. Pay attention to all possible causes of events and behavior to take full advantage of the *Action Hacks* (p. 153).

4. **Mindful Hack**—*Focus on the process of goal attainment, not only the outcome.*

The details

My daughter and I have traveled the world together, but whenever we arrived in an exotic or intriguing foreign location, she bombarded me with questions about *where we were going next*. It made me so mad that Rebecca seemed uninterested in the present. She always wanted to know when we were leaving to go to another city, what day we were going home—nothing about where we were or what we were doing at the time. Rebecca was very focused on the *outcomes* of our adventures (and what she could share on social media) rather than on the immediate experience. Let me tell you, there's nothing like marveling at the Sistine Chapel's ceiling or the majestic Egyptian pyramids while being asked, "Dad, where are we going for lunch?"

Rebecca's orientation toward the future illustrates the need for the *Mindful Hack*, which asks you to intentionally focus on the present moment. When we pay attention to the present, we automatically focus on what we are doing and to the strategies we are using, which can determine the outcomes we achieve. Focusing on the present shifts our attention away from the *outcome*—the end state—to the *process* of goal attainment. The *Mindful Hack* allows us to look back on a success, analyze the methods we used, and repeat what worked.

Why it works

Focusing your attention on the process of goal achievement is valuable for learning, performance, and sustained motivation. When we consciously monitor what we are doing, we can adjust the strategies we use based on our progress. If we are moving along fine toward our goals, we can keep going as we are; if we're not on track, we can change course. Mindful attention also allows us to monitor the state of our motivation while we work, letting us see when our effort is declining. If we are aware of the peaks and valleys of our motivation, we can adjust our effort accordingly, saving our best efforts for the hardest parts of a task.

There are mental and physical advantages to this focus on process. Physiologically, when we look forward to a positive learning or performance outcome, our bodies react in the same way they do when we anticipate a monetary reward: the anticipation triggers the production of the neurotransmitter dopamine, which produces feelings of satisfaction and contentment. In other words, it is the thrill of the chase (the process) that motivates us and triggers dopamine production, not the reaching of the goal. Mentally, when we focus on process, we feel a sense of accomplishment and confidence as we make progress on our task, creating a recurring cycle of achievement, dopamine production, and feelings of efficacy and satisfaction.

Application

The *Mindful Hack* is most useful when we are learning new things. Students, seminar attendees, and workshop participants sometimes focus on outcomes (achieving certain grades or gaining certifications) rather than on the process of gaining knowledge and enhancing competence. Learning is most successful when students monitor their improvement; *how* the learning takes place can be as important as *what* is being learned. For example, students might get the right answer to a mathematics problem in several different ways, but focusing on *how* they solved the problem can help them transfer those effective problem-solving methods to other problems.

Process focus is useful at the organizational level too. For example, many companies use incentive and bonus plans to motivate higher sales or better productivity—financial rewards that are determined by achievement. But the high achievers' methods are not often examined or shared with other employees, although this would probably increase the company's overall productivity. Using the *Mindful Hack* promotes individual accountability for actions and outcomes and shows others how to replicate award-winning performances, as well as helping to identify which organizational policies and practices support or detract from goal achievement.

5. **Calibration Hack**—*Do not overestimate or underestimate your ability.*

The details

It happens every single day. We make plans, but they invariably come up short. This happens in part because we perform better in our minds than in reality—we overestimate our abilities. For example, I miscalculate how long it will take me to drive in city traffic *every single time*, and I always arrive late to wherever I'm going (darn my unquenchable optimism!). Corporations fall victim to this blunder too—software and game developers are notorious for fudging overly ambitious target dates by releasing products that are not ready for prime time. Governments are infamously poor predictors, underestimating project budgets and resource requirements and overestimating project benefits. Successful estimation requires excellent *calibration*, or the ability to precisely gauge the skill, ability, or effort needed to complete a task. In other words, to be well-calibrated, your perceptions of a goal's timelines, required effort, and necessary skills must align with the *realities* of the task. For various estimations—how long it will take to drive to work, how much time and effort it will take to put together your new 425-piece IKEA couch, or how much a book about motivation should cost—myside bias (p. 58) is always lurking, waiting to pounce.

The *Calibration Hack* asks you to take a realistic, objective, and conservative approach to estimating specific task requirements. In the long term, good calibration and realistic estimates are more likely to lead to successful outcomes, because we know how much effort we must invest to complete a task. Conversely, poor calibration—when people believe they have more skills and talent than they actually do—is more likely to lead to failure. The problem of poor calibration is especially damaging for newly graduated university students entering the workforce. In a recent survey, graduates were asked to assess their own performance on important workplace skills like teamwork, communication, and tech knowledge. Students' self-assessments were compared to the same assessments completed by their employers. Students evaluated their skills at *double* the proficiency level that their bosses did! Another Gallup Poll found that only 11 percent of business leaders strongly agreed that students have the appropriate skills and competencies necessary for job success. And many people go through their entire lives with an inflated sense of their abilities that is never punctured by their actual mediocre performance. The *Calibration Hack* will help you accurately assess your real strengths and weaknesses so you can perform at your peak.

YouTube video: Calibration

Why it works
So, what's the big deal if you have a little extra confidence that isn't actually supported by your abilities? For one thing, overconfidence means you may invest too little effort to successfully accomplish a task. Poor calibration in a college calculus class may lead students to skip homework or not study for exams. Poor calibration while driving—thinking that you can text and drive perfectly well—kills about five thousand people per year. Poor calibration can also turn you into a jerk. If you calibrate yourself against the wrong benchmarks, poor calibration can lead to narcissism, overblown ego, and an obsession with appearances over results. Your calibration benchmarks should be objective standards, not other people. Later, the

Anchor Hack (p. 87) will show you how to make useful, objective comparisons that can improve your performance.

People who overestimate their abilities may set unrealistic goals that they are unlikely to reach. The *Calibration Hack*, with its focus on objectivity, helps you establish goals that are both realistic and challenging. Accurate calibration produces all kinds of positive outcomes: stress reduction, fewer reported depression symptoms, and overall higher optimism about life experiences. Precise evaluation contributes to more efficient and effective learning (because less energy is spent on anxiety); and better sustained commitment to your realistic goals (you retain motivation and interest and avoid investing far more effort than you'd planned).

Application

The best time to use the *Calibration Hack* is when you are starting a project or learning something new. I wish I had known the

Happy to rent a boat, not a bank

Calibration Hack years ago, when I started my (lifelong) project of learning Italian. During my first trip to Italy, I couldn't understand why people were giving me strange looks as I gabbed away in my one-semester college Italian—until I realized I was pronouncing everything wrong. In retrospect, my overconfidence about my language proficiency helped me make a fool of myself (I tried to rent a bank—*banca*—instead of a boat—*barca*—for a day). In those days, I was poorly calibrated in two different languages!

Work tasks are the best showcase for your abilities, but people too often over-project and under-perform. Telling your boss you will have something done and then coming up short is slow career suicide. If you fall short, supervisors don't remember your skills or your potential; they remember your missed deadlines and broken promises. Whenever you are asked to project future performance, use the *Calibration Hack*, especially when you have limited past success to use as an indicator of future performance. But don't underestimate your proficiency if you do have the necessary skills; under-calibration is linked to attending to the wrong aspects of a task and to underuse of self-monitoring skills.

6. **Stereo Hack**—*Group members have diverse motives and may intentionally violate expectations.*

The details

There are almost as many stereotypes in this world as there are weird people living in Florida. Stereotyping is flawed thinking that ascribes traits commonly associated with a group to all members of the group. Although the most common and damaging stereotypes are based on ethnicity and race, people can also be inappropriately categorized based on other characteristics: smoking preference, waist size, music taste, hair color, age, or intelligence. Stereotyping is a form of mental classification, and it happens because people look for predictable, reliable patterns of behavior (p. 55) to gauge their own actions against. But stereotypes don't work as behavior guides, because all people in a group do not act in one way. In fact, research reveals that behavior is more stable between groups than within groups. Our routine, normal behavior changes day to day because the motives and emotions that drive it change. Avoid stereotypical judgments about people, because you will likely be wrong.

But members of some groups *expect* to be stereotyped, and may even adopt a form of self-stereotyping to maintain their difference from the dominant culture or to protest group inequality. When people act in ways stereotypical of race, gender, ethnicity, age, occupation, or anything else, they are showing that they value being part of the stereotyped group more than they value fitting in with the dominant culture. This is where the *Stereo Hack* comes in. This Hack teaches us that people sometimes deliberately portray stereotypes that don't necessarily represent their true motives. When we can use the *Stereo Hack* to identify self-stereotypical behavior, we can more clearly identify a person's true motives.

Why it works
Without the *Stereo Hack*, you might misinterpret behaviors that are simply protecting the person's ego. The self-stereotyping person wants to feel at ease with how they fit, psychologically and sociologically, into the dominant culture. It's as if a mask-wearer began to believe that the mask depicted their real self. People who self-stereotype believe social hierarchies and racism will never change. Acting in stereotypical ways reduces their stress and insecurity about circumstances they see as oppressive and beyond their control.

When people embrace the stereotypes ascribed to them by an unjust society, they generate positive emotion; they see themselves as capable and competent individuals in an inequitable world. This is a form of depersonalization that shifts attention away from the self and onto the perceived injustice. Savvy motivational hackers will see the strong influence of culture on behavior; they will realize that people behaving in stereotypical ways are dissatisfied with their perceptions and are seeking ways to enhance their own motivational and emotional well-being.

Application

Even if you don't know many people who self-stereotype in this way, this Hack can help us understand other behaviors we encounter. For example, some people withhold effort in academic or work projects because they think they will fail anyway, and any effort would be wasted. The *Stereo Hack* is most useful with people who feel disadvantaged by society's rules and regulations and who perceive themselves as outliers in the dominant culture. People who reject the dominant culture often align psychologically with their in-group, and their in-group identity influences their behavior more than any other factor. But these people may genuinely want to form alliances with all people, and may feel anxious or uncomfortable. Knowing the *Stereo Hack* can help you promote harmony despite individual differences.

7. **Anchor Hack**—*Identify your personal benchmarks to maximize effort.*

The details

I have a friend—let's call him Morty. Morty is charming, intelligent, and *annoying*. He is charming because of his sense of humor, intelligent because he is knowledgeable about diverse topics, and annoying because he compares himself to anyone he can find. We all compare ourselves to others, of course. But Morty is fixated on comparing his accomplishments to other people's. Morty does fine by established standards (he has a 3.8 college GPA), but he prefers to evaluate his own accomplishments against those of friends, relatives, and coworkers. He gets miffed when other people accomplish anything, even have babies, get married, or celebrate anniversaries—events he considers predictable and mundane. In other words, Morty's not a lot of fun to be friends with on social media.

We all engage in comparison, but Morty's method—comparing his performance to other people's—is only one way to do it. Some of us compare ourselves to our own internal guidelines and goals by besting our own past performance, as I did when I started running (p. 29). People in this category are content if they are better, faster, or accomplish more than last time. Others use societal benchmarks, called *standards*, to set performance targets. These standards include things like speed limits, passing rates, or company- or team-determined goals. The *Anchor Hack* helps you figure out the standards being used for comparisons. When you know the comparison standard, you are in a much better position to roll out appropriate *Action Hacks* (p. 153) to accomplish your performance goals or help others reach theirs.

Why it works

Points of comparison, or *anchors*, set boundaries for people's goals and behaviors. Knowing which anchor someone usually uses helps determine how to change undesirable behaviors. For example, people may compare themselves to others  if standards are not clear and explicit enough, or they may do it to justify their own behavior, or they might want to boost their egos by finding someone else inferior—three very different motivations for the same comparison anchor (p.

YouTube video: Anchor

68). What matters most is detecting the *type* of comparison anchor people use, because comparison methods align with specific goal attainment strategies. As you might have surmised, comparing ourselves with others often doesn't produce the same level of competence as comparing ourselves to a defined standard.

Social comparisons can motivate improvement, but only one type: upward comparisons. Comparing yourself to someone you perceive as superior can prompt you to improve your own performance (always play tennis against someone better than you, if you want to improve). Downward comparisons generally just make you feel better about your current state, rather than motivating you to improve. These downward comparisons are used by people who lack confidence or self-esteem and who worry about what others think of them. Downward comparison feels good because when we think others are inferior to us, our brains produce the feel-good neurotransmitter dopamine, enhancing our perception of well-being.

It's best to avoid making social comparisons yourself. Either type of social comparison—upward or downward—can have bad effects: if you come up short in the comparison, your self-esteem plummets, and your motivation drops like a stone. This can short-circuit your attempts to set challenging goals or attempt difficult tasks others successfully pull off (like getting a high-paying job or earning a college degree). It may heighten your fear of failure. Social comparison can produce apathy and lack of effort—after all, you can't look bad in comparison to others if you do nothing. No action, no show, no ego blow.

Application

The *Anchor Hack* is especially important for managers, teachers, and parents, because people who use social comparison as their anchor must be managed differently than people who use past performance or standards as their anchor. Social comparers fear falling short, and they may need extra incentives to act assertively or to try new things. Since social comparison influences self-perception, when social comparers underachieve (in reality or in their imaginations), they experience anxiety, ruminate over their inadequacies, and think less clearly as a result. To counteract their worrying, work with the person to set clear, measurable goals that are achievable with reasonable sustained effort.

The *Anchor Hack* is also useful in organizational contexts. Like individuals, some companies deliberately choose to stay out of the limelight; they don't want to be seen as industry leaders. These types of companies compare themselves to other successful firms. While there are no psychological or motivational consequences for companies that use this strategy, the tactic can limit the growth and innovation of the individuals who make up the organization. Workers may see little value in being creative when success means imitating competitors. For example, many academic institutions take a reactive position, only making changes when they look bad compared to peer institutions. This reactionary approach fosters complacency (p. 45); people in the organization lose their sense of initiative, not acting unless they are explicitly directed by higher-ups. This reactionary approach is one reason why both academic and corporate organizations don't always thrive. The organization sometimes doesn't realize it should change its benchmarks until it is too late to recover from organizational apathy.

8. Selling Hack—*Be aware of subtle persuasion tactics designed to change your beliefs.*

The details

As we've discussed, everyone tends to think that their own way of viewing and navigating the world is the best way. We all have our own deeply entrenched set of motivational beliefs formed over a lifetime. These beliefs usually help us achieve our goals; although we don't succeed every time with our chosen methods, we have enough success that we develop comfortable patterns of behavior, and these define who we are to the external world. This variety of experiences and beliefs is valuable in some situations (brainstorming solutions to problems) and fine in many more (deciding what kind of takeout to order—everyone's food preferences are valid for them, and we rarely argue with this kind of preference). But there is a dark side to the diversity and variety of ideas: we think our own ideas are superior, and we try to persuade others to think like we do.

The *Selling Hack* is a bullshit detector that automatically activates when people try to sell you their ideas like they were selling used cars—when they try to pressure you into buying their opinions and beliefs. Guileful, persuasive convincers have lots of strategies to get your attention. Some make outlandish claims using colorful language or technical jargon. I tell my students, "My motivation class will contribute more to your life success than all of your other courses combined!"—a passionate declaration that is completely unsupported by evidence. Some try to exploit the *Buy Later Hack* (p. 74) with emotional appeals by shifting the burden of proof onto you, saying that if you can't deliver a crushing refutation, their opinion must be correct. Others shift the focus from the content of the claim to the reputation of the claim-maker—if you question these used idea sellers' opinions, they react like you've insulted them, their mother, and all the kittens on the internet. There are plenty of other shifty sales techniques, too, but the *Selling Hack* can help you thwart them all.

Why it works

Let's face it: if you're naïve, you can be manipulated. Even if you're not especially naïve, you almost certainly fall prey sometimes to social influence, obedience, and group conformity (look up the famous Milgram experiment, in which perfectly nice, normal people delivered increasingly intense electric shocks to other perfectly nice, normal people because nobody wanted to be the first to refuse instructions from authority figures). The *Stereo Hack* (p. 85) taught us that people can behave in ways that seem inconsistent with their underlying beliefs. The *Selling Hack* takes this a little farther: it tells us that people act differently based on social expectations and other people's influence. For example, we often do things out of a sense of reciprocal social obligation—we might

YouTube video: Selling

tip a server despite bad service if they complimented us on our meal choice. And we sometimes agree with others *even when we know they are wrong* because we need to feel liked and be accepted as part of a group. We literally *need* this; the body responds to feelings of emotional rejection the same way it does to physical pain. Rejection hurts just like a cut or a burn.

We are especially vulnerable to used idea sellers in positions of authority. As Milgram's experiment showed, when directed by someone in authority, people will inflict pain on others. People are more likely to pick up trash on the street when told to by someone in a security guard uniform than when ordered to by someone in street clothes. Lawyers and law enforcement officials routinely get confession to crimes that people did not commit—appeals from these authority figures to the innocent person's fear or sense of obligation are terrifyingly effective. The *Selling Hack* can be used for evil or for good; people can be convinced to do just about anything—overpaying for products, committing crimes, buying motivation books—through the power of persuasion.

Application

Use the *Selling Hack* when someone is trying to persuade you to align your views with theirs. Knowing the persuader's intentions and motives lets you choose effective countering strategies—you can often turn the persuader's own tactics back on them. First, try an emotional appeal to gain attention. Next, think of the quality and integrity of the message you are sending, and do your homework on the facts. Follow your strong message by making the person feel obligated to follow your lead because of your integrity, intelligence, and sense of fair play. Then ask the person for an outlandish concession, which they will likely reject. Finally, hit them hard with a smaller, reasonable request—your likelihood of a positive response to the second request will be considerably increased.

The *Selling Hack* is especially helpful in situations where a group is making a decision. Initially agree with the group to gain the confidence and trust of group members. Once trust is gained, plant a seed of doubt about the group's opinion on an issue. Tell the group that diverse opinions are valuable and that creative solutions are more likely to flow when individuality prevails over groupthink. Open minds by using the *Selling Hack* to your benefit—but be aware that others may be using the same strategies on you!

●

9. Cap Hack—*Remove artificial success barriers that stall personal growth.*

The details

There is one thing that aggravates a professor more than anything else: students. Not all students, of course—just the ones who shoot themselves in the foot. Lack of academic success doesn't have much to do with ability; it comes from restrictive self-perceptions and beliefs that artificially limit students' growth. When I ask my students, "How many of you believe that, no matter how much you study or how hard you try, you will not improve at mathematics?" about 60 percent of my students—*graduate* students!— raise their hands. They are wrong, of course, and I tell them so. They can learn whatever they are willing to let themselves learn.

Most people don't know this, but there is no limit to potential knowledge gains; expertise is developed through the investment of effort and time. People who self-limit have voluntarily picked up a ball and chain, but this imaginary weight can be dropped by using the *Cap Hack*. Once you acknowledge that you've imposed arbitrary limits on your own learning, you can choose productive skill-building strategies to increase your knowledge and ability—and not only in academics. Many of us won't take social risks; we believe we can only be so personable, and the thought of rejection makes us anxious, turning us into our own worst enemies. But the *Cap Hack* releases you from all kinds of self-imposed limits, freeing you up to use the forthcoming *Action Hacks* (p. 153).

Why it works

People have two kinds of beliefs about capability. Some believe that there are barriers to success, either erected by society or self-imposed; this belief, which we will call the *obstructed* view, justifies their lack of development. People accept their supposed limitations, restrictions that they think won't shift no matter how much or how intensely they try (remember my students who believed they could not get better at math). Others seem to already be using the *Cap*

Hack—these people take the *unobstructed* view of personal development, believing that people lack skills or knowledge only because they lack enough exposure, opportunity, or effective practice time. Once the obstructions are removed, growth follows.

Skills do not develop spontaneously once we remove our restricted beliefs, of course, but expertise is a function of opportunity and time, not of ability. In reality, almost all skills and abilities can improve through dedicated practice. When people commit to skill building and work with a competent coach or instructor, knowledge gains almost always follow. This means that no matter what hand you are dealt in life, you can exchange your cards for a different set; winning from a new hand simply requires you to suspend your restrictive beliefs and work harder to achieve your goals. Know which strategies to use, apply the right strategies at the right time, and continue to practice the skill over time; you *will* improve.

Application

The *Cap Hack* comes into play when we need to learn something new—traditional learning in school, training sessions, athletics, or continuing education workshops—or whenever we might doubt our abilities. The Hack is especially important in high-pressure situations with other people around; performing in front of others can add to performance anxiety. (If you've ever practiced a speech in front of a mirror and then choked in front of an audience, you know what I mean.)

The key to the *Cap Hack* is admitting three realities to yourself. First, acknowledge that *all skills develop through learning*; no one is born with ability. Second, *you can't be great at everything*; expertise across several areas is very rare (and is mostly found in people with bloated egos or too much time on their hands). Third—and this one is most important—*you must allow yourself to learn*; don't assume a defensive posture toward learning. Jump right in. Improve, and show yourself (and others) your unlimited potential.

●

10. Belief Hack—*Skill is necessary, but self-confidence propels achievement.*

The details

When I committed to the full-time PhD program in Las Vegas (p. 41), I was anxious, to say the least. I gave up a lucrative career for an assistantship job typically reserved for starry-eyed twenty-somethings—I thought I would be the oldest student in the program. Embarrassing, right? But even though I had plenty of reasons to be worried, I really didn't care. This changed radically when I was told nine days before the application deadline that I needed to take the Graduate Record Exam (GRE), a standardized entrance exam with algebra and logic problems that I hadn't thought about in twenty-two years. I was petrified! I arrived at the testing center and was led to a computer. I was told that the three-hour test had four sections; one didn't count, but was being used to test whether the questions were suitable to become part of future exams. Of course, the crafty test torturers didn't tell me *which* section didn't count. My heart pounded.

YouTube video: Belief

As the questions appeared on the screen, I panicked—these questions seemed much harder than the ones I had been studying feverishly for the past nine days. My stomach started to churn. I started randomly guessing at answers. My performance and motivation to succeed plummeted. Now I was really in trouble. I had already shut down my business and moved my stuff; now I was going to make a fool of myself by flunking out before I even started. I wish that I'd known about the *Belief Hack* back then. The *Belief Hack* says that when you have the necessary skills and knowledge, the strength of your belief in your ability to succeed makes the difference between success and failure. When skills are equal, the person with the most confidence consistently outperforms their low-confidence peers. On GRE day, despite my ability, pretty much anyone could have bested my performance.

Why it works

Perhaps no other motivation principle has as much rock-solid scientific evidence supporting it as the power of confidence beliefs. When we are committed to a plan and have basic topic knowledge, we often reach our goals. If we believe we have the intellectual horsepower, motivation, and strategies to produce the results we want, we pursue our goals relentlessly. Self-doubt breeds failure even when we have the necessary skills. People who use the *Belief Hack* have resilience, perseverance, and resourcefulness when they encounter the obstacles that crop up with just about every challenging task. And people who use the *Belief Hack* are also more likely to ask for help when they need it—a fast-forward goal attainment strategy.

Users of this Hack take a radically different approach to learning than self-doubters. Belief hackers use a greater variety of strategies because they have confidence that they will create a successful outcome. They don't downgrade goals or lose momentum when encountering obstacles; they see obstacles as part of the learning and performance process, and they power through temporary motivational lulls because failure is just not a potential outcome. Most importantly, users of the *Belief Hack* make good choices and are not afraid of a challenge; they seek out the toughest courses and the most challenging careers, respond well under pressure, and are frequently in better health than their self-doubting peers.

Application

The effectiveness of the *Belief Hack* varies by task. For one thing, your confidence levels fluctuate based on how familiar the task is, how complex the required skill set is, and how much experience you need to pull off a success. And the *Belief Hack* isn't magic; believing in your success won't automatically create the outcome you want. The *Belief Hack* requires a challenge that you can reasonably meet. The *Belief Hack* is especially useful for any performance or learning task that provides you with feedback that lets you monitor your progress: tasks like computer-based learning, athletic challenges, and performances that involve other people all offer useful feed-back that can increase your confidence. And definitely keep this Hack in mind when you are teaching others. Remember that effective teaching isn't just about teaching concrete steps or principles, but about teaching habits of mind that produce success. Task success is not only a function of knowledge. It is deeply entwined with our beliefs about ourselves and our capabilities.

11. Rest Stop Hack—*Motivation is depletable. Breaks are essential for optimal results.*

The details

Expecting yourself to work at peak intensity and effort over long periods of time is a recipe for failure. It is unrealistic to imagine that motivation follows different rules than other elements of human performance. Of course, many of the so-called motivational gurus say it does (remember, they need to create self-doubt in you to keep you buying their books). Motivational huckster Tony Robbins says on his website, "The path to success is to take massive determined action." In real life, if you undertake "massive determined action," you are likely to deplete your motivation and end up exhausted or burned out. Remember the old story of the tortoise and the hare.

YouTube video:
Rest Stop

The *Rest Stop Hack* works on the same principles as physical exercise. Physically, we perform at our best when we are in good health, rested, and well nourished. As we expend energy, we get increasingly tired, and eventually reach a state of exhaustion. Any knowledgeable coach recognizes when an athlete needs rest, some time to regenerate depleted energy, and maybe a drink. Motivational effort works the same way. Recovery times for motivation differ across people and tasks, but to keep your motivational performance high, you need time for rest and renewal after sustained effort. If you have ever been on a diet, worked consistently on a research paper, or even taken a long vacation with your family, you may have found yourself saying, "I need a break." To be successful in the long term, you should use the *Rest Stop Hack* on your own timetable. Don't allow others to dictate your work and rest patterns. You are the best judge of how and when you work at your peak.

Why it works

The *Rest Stop Hack* is based on two sound scientific principles. First, recall from the *Mindful Hack* (p. 80) that monitoring our ongoing performance lets us choose strategies to help us meet our goals. But ongoing self-monitoring requires prolonged attention, and it is hard work to sustain our motivation over time. We usually start off with a bang because we are all fired up, but as we make progress, our energy slowly trickles away. The sustained effort needed to control negative behavior over the long term— the kind of willpower needed to monitor obsessive behaviors like video game addictions, alcohol abuse, and eating disorders—is especially likely to deplete motivation. The more time that passes, the more depleted our ability to regulate our behavior, and the more likely we will lose motivation to resist temptation.

Second, whenever we expend mental or emotional effort, our bodies expend energy. Blood glucose levels drop when we exert ourselves. When the body's glucose level drops, our ability to control our behavior drops too. Baseline glucose levels and glucose consumption vary across individuals, but sooner or later we all expend enough emotional or mental effort that we need more glucose. The more pressure we perceive, the more glucose we use. Of course, the easiest way to fix this is to take a break and eat something— that's the usual way of using the *Rest Stop Hack*. But if you can't manage a break, there's another way. We can override our need for glucose replenishment if we *believe* we aren't expending much energy. In high-pressure situations, you can also use the *Rest Stop Hack* by telling yourself you aren't tired, even if you are.

Application

The *Rest Stop Hack* will work as well for physically demanding tasks as for psychologically demanding ones. This Hack was especially useful for me when writing this book (and after arguing with my children). It took me years to realize I only write well (a self-perception) when I have plenty of energy. My productivity (and the quality of my writing) after three hours of intense, continuous writing is abysmal. I need breaks! Before I discovered the *Rest Stop Hack*, I used to believe that taking a break or a nap was a sign of motivational weakness and lack of commitment. Now I realize that the best strategy is to stop and get something to eat or lie down for half an hour when I'm spent. In the long run, I perform better and am more productive when I use the Hack than when I push through these motivational dips.

Your best use of the *Rest Stop Hack* depends on you. Don't let anyone else—other motivational hackers, friends, partners, or parents—tell you that what works for them will work for you. Part of the *Rest Stop Hack* is accepting that pausing is a productive strategy—not a reason to feel guilty or lazy. Listen to *your* body and *your* mind, because you know better than anyone else what works best for you. Ignore people who tell you to never let up or to always give 100 percent. Neither science nor practice can argue with the *Rest Stop Hack*. Even God rested on the seventh day, and you should too.

●

Awareness Hacks focus our attention on things we should be thinking about as we decide to act on a specific motivational challenge. Awareness primes us to consider what may be interfering with our clear, accurate interpretation of the evidence we see. By using the Hacks described in this section, the motivational hacker can objectively decide which strategies and tips are most likely to lead to the desired result. Ultimately, mastering the *Awareness Hacks* means you'll make decisions about behavior—yours and others—without false or misleading information, bias, or gaps in your knowledge. Now that you have mastered motivational myths and learned the red flags about awareness, it's time to make some decisions. In the next section, you'll move forward by using *Choice Hacks* to guide the *direction* and *intensity* of your motivated effort.

CHAPTER FOUR

Choice Hacks

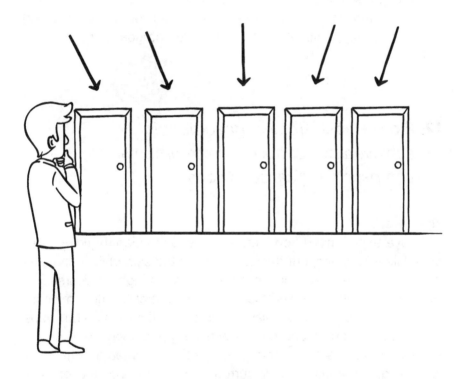

THE CHOICES WE MAKE lead to behaviors that represent us—our choices show the rest of the world how we think about ourselves, personally and professionally. The mechanics of choice are often routine, but there are some choices that we enthusiastically pursue, wholeheartedly enjoy, and share with pride. *Choice Hacks* build on *Awareness Hacks* (p. 71): decision-making is often guided by intuitive and automatic thinking, operating below the level of active consciousness, and includes habitual behavior patterns formed over a lifetime. The goal for this chapter is to determine which factors we consider (or should consider) when choosing personal preferences, targeted goals, or motivated behavior.

12. Flow Hack—*Total engagement is achieved by controlling environmental and psychological conditions.*

The details

You have experienced flow before. It's easy to identify flow in others while it happens, but detecting flow in the self while it happens is impossible—when you become aware enough of yourself to evaluate your attention and focus, you slip out of the flow mindset, and flow inevitably ends. Maybe you are in flow now—but oops, you thought about it, and now flow has slipped away. People who experience flow are immersed, completely engaged in what they are doing, oblivious to their surroundings, and unaware of time. Concentration lapses caused by assessing feelings, gauging task progress, or evaluating your motivational state do not exist during flow. The flow state might seem mystical, but it's not rare. Most of us experience flow almost every day.

You may be thinking that flow is artificially induced, achieved by swallowing a miracle pill or practicing some ancient ritual of spiritual awakening. But in reality, flow happens during many routine activities and tasks. Flow is most frequently reported during driving. Other instances of flow occur during work—perhaps when you are fully absorbed in a project or when you try to amuse yourself by completing a boring task in a record amount of time. Many athletes report experiencing flow. They call this being "in the zone," and it happens during intense competition, when the athlete's mind focuses on nothing but the competition in the moment and the overwhelming desire to win. Surprisingly, people report fewer instances of flow during leisure activities. This is because play often lacks significant challenge, an important requirement for the flow experience.

Why it works

Highly motivated performers—people who are often completely engrossed in their work—detest having their concentration interrupted. These interruptions can be internal ones: anxiety due to lack of task confidence, emotional distractions (anger, sadness, or excitement), or motivational lapses (moments of self-doubt when it seems that the task is more challenging than we can handle). Cognitive interference can also come from outside the self: uncomfortable temperatures, children screaming, dogs barking, or lawn mowers rumbling can all serve to pull you out of flow. The first step toward flow is controlling these intrusions, either

YouTube video:
Flow

by physically removing the intrusion or by ignoring it. But a quiet mind and environment don't guarantee flow. For a performer to experience flow, the task must also meet certain conditions: it should be at least marginally interesting, it should be reasonably challenging, and it should provide some form of performance feedback. When personal, environmental, and task factors line up properly and the performer wants to engage in and complete the task at hand, the stage is set for flow.

As outlined in the *Mindful Hack* (p. 80), we perform best when we see value in the task and in meeting our task goals. We reach the temporary bliss of flow only when the right conditions are in place and only for as long as concentration remains uninterrupted. If the task gets harder—hard enough that we doubt ourselves—flow stops until we have adjusted to the more strenuous conditions. People often experience flow while playing video games because the player explicitly chooses the degree of difficulty; if the challenge level is too high or too low, flow is compromised. When all psychological and biological systems are synchronized, the flow state happens automatically and produces superior performance that continues until conditions change.

Application

How can you achieve flow to maximize your performance? First, pick a familiar task (this is why flow is a *Choice Hack*), then kick it up a notch. In other words, take your performance to the next level: read a book that requires your focused concentration to understand, have a deeply engaging conversation with someone you adore or admire, or take a jog down the street with a family pet or human of your choice. Repeatedly practice the task until you achieve a state of satisfaction and mastery—what psychologists refer to as *automaticity*, which occurs when you can complete the task with little effort or conscious thought. Automaticity is the reason many people report flow during driving. Experienced drivers drive without thinking about the actual mechanics.

You can also deliberately structure tasks to induce flow. Try making a boring or repetitive task more interesting by testing your performance limits. See if you can mow the lawn faster than you did last time. If speed is not your need, challenge yourself to mow your lawn into a Donald Trump comb-over (maybe you'll bond with your conservative neighbors). If all else fails, sink yourself into your favorite book, movie, or leisure activity, but only if it is stimulating enough to warrant your undivided attention. Or you can deeply engage with a romantic partner, or engross yourself in an intellectual debate with a formidable opponent. Achieving flow is a highly personal experience, but when everything is in place and you reach flow, it almost guarantees optimal performance.

13. **Investment Hack**—*Valuation determines how much effort we are willing to devote to a task.*

The details

I have a great offer for you, a deal so easy and lucrative that you don't need to worry about the *Wake-Up* or *Buy Later Hacks* (p. 72–74) I described earlier. I want to feature your picture on the cover of my next book, and I'll pay you ten thousand dollars to pose for a few pictures. Sound like a good deal? Some of you might be thinking "Yes!" right now. If you're hiding from the law, though, you're probably not interested. It wouldn't be worth it. But the rest of you are still in, right? Is the price high enough for you to give up your privacy? High enough that you don't mind being associated with someone like me? Oh, yes, I forgot to mention the title of my next book is *The 100 Stupidest Humans*. Are you still interested in the cover opportunity? Would you do it for twenty thousand dollars? Two hundred thousand? Two million?

Many of you were probably interested in the initial offer, but as you learned additional details and thought about what it would mean to your life, your enthusiasm probably waned. From a psychological perspective, you evaluated the outcomes and costs associated with my offer. In evaluating how to invest our time and effort, we decide to pursue a task only when it aligns with our values, behaviors, interests, and self-views. In my example above, the decision to pose for my book cover needed to be aligned with your beliefs and interests. If you were starving, you would probably accept my offer under any terms and conditions. If you were rich, it would seem like a waste of time no matter how high the offer went. I probably lost the people with highly negative self-views and low competency beliefs (p. 134) when I mentioned the book title—these people don't want to be associated with stupidity. People without insecurity about their intellectual prowess might agree to do it for enough money; it wouldn't cause them negative self-impressions no matter how much public mockery they received as a result. The final decision would, of course, be based on a combination of factors (as explained by the *Integration Hack*, p. 77), but once you have mastered the *Investment Hack*, you will better understand your own decisions and predict the choices others will make.

Why it works

We either want to move toward or away from a task, person, or event. Moving toward a target shows *approach* motivation, and moving away reveals an *avoidance* motivation. To approach a target, we must have some sort of incentive; this is called the payoff. Payoffs are highly personalized based on what people value, but they always represent some sort of perceived gain. The gain can be tangible, like a paycheck, a degree, or a socially satisfying experience—anything the person decides is interesting and enjoyable. Multiple factors determine which payoff provides the best incentive; your payoff may seem like garbage to someone else, and vice versa. And the value of an incentive fluctuates, both within and across individuals. Motivation can be unpredictable.

When we make choices, we conduct a series of *value calculations*, which in many cases happens below the level of active consciousness. First, we mentally evaluate the *importance* of completing a task or engaging with someone. Second, we assess how much *enjoyment* we are likely to get from doing something, whether for work or for fun. Some people and tasks make us feel like psychological prisoners, and others are mentally invigorating. Third, we assess how *useful* mastering a task or engaging with an individual will be—we consider how the activity will advance our short- and long-term goals. We often (begrudgingly) do things we'd rather not do because they will move us toward our long-term goals. This *usefulness* aspect of choice is why we are willing to devote years of time and effort to education. We hope for an eventual payoff, both in money and in social status, from our degrees.

Last, value calculations involve assessment of the *costs* associated with decisions. Costs include the inability to perform other, more desirable tasks, the amount of effort that must be invested to successfully complete the task, and the social circumstances around task completion (or task failure). If you are like me, you might avoid a task whose consequences for failure are too high. I remember quite vividly not wanting to play the outfield in Little League (p. 13). It was because the potential costs were deal-breakers; I expected embarrassment and shame from watching balls bounce off my head or out of my glove. The takeaway here is that the *Investment Hack* is a highly personal calculation. Just like when we invest money, before we commit to a significant deposit of effort and time, we always prefer to know the likely investment return.

Application

The *Investment Hack* can be used to evaluate choices about careers, relationships, or major expenses. It can also be used to understand, persuade, and influence others. First, carefully evaluate options and determine whether your choice will lead to your long-term success and well-being. People often make decisions they regret because they act impulsively, considering only immediate outcomes rather than projecting longer-term consequences. Don't only project the benefits of pursuing a target; also project the consequences if the choice were *not* made. In other words,

YouTube video:
Investment

don't evaluate only action; also consider the impact of inaction. For example, I know for sure that Dwayne the Road King (p. 15) made a deliberate choice to avoid the one-dollar bridge toll because he thought we would admire his moxie. Too bad Dwayne didn't also consider what would happen if he just paid the toll. In retrospect, that projection would have saved him $249.00 and an awful lot of ribbing from us.

The *Investment Hack* can also be useful to help you understand how others make decisions. If you know how people evaluate task value, interest, enjoyment, and usefulness, you can often persuade them to consider other options or new information as they decide. People act or don't act based on the perceived consequences of their effort. By using projection strategies that provide clear answers about a task's value, you can motivate a reluctant or inexperienced performer. Renee should have used the *Investment Hack* on me to convince me that going to college was worthwhile (p. 17). Instead, she made me go because she said so. If she had shown me evidence that people who earn a degree make more money over a lifetime, or asked me what kind of career I wanted and explained why I needed a degree to get it, or even convinced me that attending college would land me a beautiful, smart girlfriend, she would have been more persuasive, and I might have invested more effort. Ultimately, persuasion works far better than force, especially when there is evidence for the task's value, interest, or practical utility.

14. Status Quo Hack—*Some people embrace consistency, others prefer change.*

The details

I have a friend named Mason. After twelve years working for a large commercial bank (you'd recognize it if I told you which one), Mason is tired of the daily corporate grind, and he decides to quit his high-paying but boring job to go into business with his wife Judy. Mason knows he wants to help other people become more financially secure, but isn't exactly sure what services his business should offer. Judy worries about Mason quitting his job because she feels more secure when they have a predictable weekly paycheck coming in, but she too wants to go into business. She supports Mason, but she feels he isn't thorough enough. She believes he hasn't considered important new-business basics like cash flow and operating expenses. Mason and Judy can't agree on which business approach is best, and the tension is creating stress in their relationship.

Mason and Judy have a problem, but what exactly is it? Neither Mason nor Judy view themselves as risk takers, but they have radically different views about how to start a business. Judy wants to know all the facts and details, while Mason is more comfortable with intuitive decisions. Judy wants to start a traditional business like tax consulting or financial planning, while Mason is seeking a novel, unconventional business solution, something exciting that hasn't been tried before. Mason wants to borrow money to get started, while Judy objects to spending cash before generating income. Mason and Judy are a classic case of competing thinking styles. Ironically, the best, most dynamic teams are made up of people with different thinking styles, but when two people have completely different approaches to regulating their motivations, it's sometimes difficult for them to collaborate effectively. In this real-life example, Mason illustrates a *promotion* orientation. He is opportunistic and has a vision that involves taking chances and risks—in his mind, nothing is a sure thing, and he loves challenge. Judy has a *prevention* focus. She likes predictability and believes the best decisions are made logically after considering all the facts. Mason and Judy don't realize that we can hack the difference between the two orientations to understand and resolve these kinds of motivational conflicts.

Why it works

People tend to view the world from one of two primary perspectives. Some of us set goals, make future projections, and view our actions as likely to lead to success. Some of us operate cautiously, worry about failed attempts, and dwell on what might go wrong if we decide to act. Although there are blended thinking styles, people tend to metaphorically view the glass as either half empty or half full. When we are optimistic, action often follows. When we are guarded and insecure, we may stagnate. It's important to recognize people's thinking styles; different approaches have profound impacts on the kinds of goals we set and the strategies we will use to accomplish them.

Promotion-oriented people thrive on seeing the results of their efforts and bask in taking credit for their accomplishments. They are highly ambitious and see themselves as dynamic risk takers who seize the moment. When asked to describe themselves, promotion people prefer labels like "change agent," "innovator," and "entrepreneur." Prevention-oriented people are more conservative and feel safe and secure when life goes according to plan. They deliberately avoid criticism and would rather be bored than try something new and fail. Prevention-oriented people cherish low-risk approaches and the status quo and tend to be motivated by psychological safety and security. These people feel best when they are saving for a rainy day and like to be referred to as "planners," "level-headed," and "reliable."

Application

The prevention/promotion explanation of motivation is useful in understanding social and organizational behavior. Socially, the prevention perspective helps us understand why people might avoid going out during nasty weather, shy away from participating in games and competitions, or spending time in crowded places like airports, bars, and sporting events. Prevention-minded people prefer socializing with a small group of close friends and often don't want to meet new people. Promotion people are adventurous and willing to try anything at least once; they are frequently described as gregarious or as the life of the party, and they are well-suited for leadership and sales roles. Promotion types volunteer for attention-getting roles and often step up to take control of situations that require planning and organization. The promotion mentality thrives on challenges and handles crises by reassuring everyone that, with their leadership, everything will be OK.

Knowing which style a person prefers can help you predict how they will behave in certain situations. The prevention/promotion orientation also helps explain why people thrive in some working environments and struggle in others. Many companies develop cultures based on a strategic vision that emphasizes either growth or preservation. Some businesses may be comfortable just staying solvent, rather than innovating. Other companies are much more aggressive and constantly look for new and better ways to enhance productivity and profits. Problems occur when personal style conflicts with organizational expectations. Promotion individuals stuck in prevention organizations become frustrated—they question authority, traditions, and existing methods, but their efforts change nothing. Similarly, the prevention person who is stuck in a promotion culture will feel overwhelmed and insecure because the decision-making process and routine behaviors in the company are often swift and intuitive. The *Status Quo Hack* can help us avoid motivation mismatches that can cause personal or professional conflict. Keep in mind that one orientation is not better than another; each orientation shines in the right situation. This Hack is diagnostic only, and it should be used to predict and understand motivational compatibility, not to prompt behavior change.

15. Humility Hack—*Allow yourself to learn by seeking constructive criticism.*

The details
The last in-person conversation I had with my late son Robert was about lifestyle perceptions. We talked about how people evaluate others' public behavior and form impressions based on what they see and hear. "Rocking Rupert," as people called him, lived in the fast lane, mostly motivated by having a good time. He enjoyed drinking with his friends and chasing after young women, and if he had the chance, he would probably have wanted to live on the yacht he wished I had, cruising the Greek islands in search of endless adventure and possibly pirate treasure. But Robert didn't have the mindset or the money to live the lifestyle he wanted. When I pointed out that perhaps he should consider other approaches to managing his time and money, we argued about individual choice and personal prerogative—basically, Robert's argument boiled

YouTube video: Humility

down to "Shut up, Dad!" Clearly, my son and I had different beliefs about leisure time and money. Why did Robert respond this way to what I intended as constructive criticism?

This argument between my son and me highlights two important considerations about feedback. First, we evaluated the message source (me) differently. To Robert, feedback from Dad felt judgmental, like criticism rather than like an offer to share my sixty years' worth of youthful idiocy and gray-haired wisdom. He couldn't separate the message from the source. This is common with parents and kids, who have a long history together; maybe if the suggestions had come from a friend or a favorite teacher, he might have listened more attentively and reacted more positively— he might have seen it not as criticism but as feedback that offered him an opportunity to improve. This brings us to the second consideration: when people receive corrective feedback, they usually respond defensively. Critical feedback can feel emotionally deflating and damaging to self-esteem, so people attempt to justify their actions. And people rarely use anything other than Type 1 thinking in reacting to criticism, which means they respond emotionally rather than rationally. For Robert, our conversation made him angry and hostile. I wish we had both known then about the *Humility Hack*, which tells us that we can only achieve optimal motivation if we allow ourselves to learn and improve from our mistakes. Using this Hack means valuing the opinion of others, actively *seeking* corrective feedback, and recognizing that all of us need help to grow. Mistakes are part of the human condition and are merely learning opportunities in disguise (p. 218).

Why it works

There are many ways to respond to feedback. People can stick their fingers in their ears and yell "LALALA I CAN'T HEAR YOU"; they can reject the message as irrelevant; or they can consider the feedback and decide to either act or not, depending on how good the advice is. Which reaction people choose depends on many different factors, including the clarity of the feedback message, the history between the people involved, how much the feedback conflicts with the receiver's existing beliefs, and whether the receiver thinks the proposed alternatives are reasonable. Most importantly, though, a person will always reject feedback if they think their current approach is just dandy. Feedback only prompts action when the receiver recognizes a compelling need to change—a motivated conclusion that Robert never reached.

The objective of the *Humility Hack* is to create a learning culture—a culture of openness to improvement and motivational change. Knowing why a person doesn't want to learn can help us persuade them to at least consider suggestions that may eventually prompt action. When a person completely rejects a clear message from a valued source, it is likely the person believes admitting to deficiencies is a sign of personal weakness, or that they are highly committed to their existing methods and beliefs. People respond to feedback based on their level of self-esteem. People with low self-esteem (which develops when there are gaps between people's accomplishments and their abilities) have difficulty accepting feedback. Although they will rarely admit it, people with low self-esteem doubt their ability to succeed, tend to avoid challenges, and fear social rejection based on their vulnerabilities. People with high self-esteem rate their abilities as matching their potential, and they are likely to accept feedback and put that feedback to work; they set aggressive performance targets, and their natural optimism tells them that they will meet those goals.

Application

The *Humility Hack* is an opportunistic Hack, meaning we must be strategic about when and how the Hack is used. To use the Hack effectively, you must figure out whether the person you'll give feedback to has high or low self-esteem. If they have low self-esteem, then you should have a conversation with them, asking questions about specific, successful actions: "When you were successful, why were you successful?" or "What strategies did you use the last time everything worked out according to your expectations?" After focusing the person on specific actions, not on self-assessments or emotion, you can offer specific *Action Hacks* (p. 153) to help them perform better and associate performance with positive emotions. This Hack focuses on the direct connection between specific actions and outcomes, helping people set themselves up for success.

People with high self-esteem are likely to view mistakes or foiled plans as an invitation to do something different. They are open to suggestions about new methods and strategies that might improve their outcomes. The high-self-esteem person often works especially hard on demanding or challenging tasks, and is resistant to self-doubt even when targets are missed; he or she likely realizes that negativity reduces motivation and success. Although people with high self-esteem don't need external encouragement to succeed, they do like positive feedback ("I know you can do this"), and it encourages them to perform at their best.

16. Inside Out Hack—*Attribution of success and failure varies; some of us take credit for success, yet blame failure on external causes.*

The details

"It was Bush's fault" was the refrain of the 2008 and 2012 United States presidential election campaigns. And like those before him, once in office, President Obama took credit for things that went well while blaming his predecessor for the stagnant economy he inherited. Although partisan pundits made a big deal about this, President Obama was not the first person to take credit for successes while blaming someone else for failures. Listen to postgame interviews, news reports about good Samaritans who save lives during natural disasters, or your partner talking about work—many of us think that we are solely responsible for our successes, but that our failures were out of our control.

As the *Integration Hack* (p. 77) showed us, we want to know *why* things happen—we seek explanations for what we see. The *Inside Out Hack* suggests that we make choices and develop beliefs based on how much control or influence we think we have over significant events, decisions, and events in our life. In psychology, we talk about *locus* of control beliefs—where people think control resides. People with an *internal* locus of control believe that they have control over their lives; these people take responsibility whether things go right *or* wrong. People who have an *external* locus of control believe forces are beyond their control—they feel subject to other people's whims and to immutable laws of nature. Not surprisingly, people with an external locus of control believe in things like luck, fatalism, and being "in the right place at the right time." These different orientations toward agency produce different approaches to setting goals and implementing plans. People with an internal locus of control make deliberate and intentional plans, then act to achieve desired outcomes. In contrast, people with an external locus of control sit back and watch the world unfold around them—this is a much more passive approach to navigating life. In other words, people *attribute* their success or failure to either themselves or to others.

Why it works

Attribution beliefs strongly influence how we make decisions and follow through on choices. People with external attributions tend to be more reserved and willing to seek advice from others. They show great restraint and will not act impulsively; they ensure that they have a well-thought-out plan that considers the consequences of their actions. People who have internal attributions are more willing to make mistakes and take risks, and are seen by others as extroverted overachievers. The internal attributors rarely sit back, because they feel compelled to take action. Some people's attributions remain stable across all types of tasks, and others' attributions change based on task. One aspect of attributions never changes: our attributions and our control beliefs determine how much work we will put toward achieving goals. If we don't believe we have much control over outcomes, then it makes little sense to invest significant effort in completing a task.

Attributions and control beliefs also influence strategy choice and outcome expectations. When people expect success, they enthusiastically pursue goals, investing effort without hesitation because they believe they will get a positive outcome. When people expect failure, they are more likely to be apathetic or to deliberately avoid tasks they see as too challenging to successfully complete. Attributions promote a corresponding set of emotions:

negative expectations create low task interest and undesirable feelings, including boredom and anxiety; positive expectations link the task with desirable emotions, such as pride and satisfaction, making sustained effort more likely.

Application

The *Inside Out Hack* is best used as a diagnostic tool to help understand why individuals set goals and use certain strategies. Knowing the locus as well as the strength of a control belief can help predict the degree of challenge an individual is willing to accept. When you know what degree of challenge is acceptable, you can determine how to best help them to task completion. People with external control beliefs need plenty of encouragement, especially evidence that directly connects effort to outcomes. People who believe they are capable of reaching goals—those with a more pronounced internal locus of control—still need support, but it can be task-focused rather than person-focused.

Here's an example of how to determine the type and extent of someone's control belief: ask them to account for their career progression. People with an elevated and internal control belief usually describe a carefully considered career plan with interim steps toward a long-term goal. People with diminished and external control beliefs usually articulate a career path determined by situational opportunities, referrals from friends, and haphazard job applications—they describe little predetermined career direction. The *Inside Out Hack* offers significant clues about what is behind important life decisions and can be highly effective in helping you predict future behavior.

●

17. Anti-Power Hack—*Never surrender your motivational power to others.*

The details

Tony Robbins's website reads "subscribe to stay motivated." If you subscribe, you can watch Robbins claim in a video that he can teach you to cure your depression by standing in a particular upright posture and moving around exactly as he instructs. Author Tamara Lowe claims that you will be instantly successful, with no limits on your achievement, once you know and understand your motivational type. On her YouTube channel, another guru, the self-proclaimed Superwoman of motivation, contends that touching your nose will give you the key to understanding your performance motivation and your ultimate success. But beware! You can't achieve your goals or reach your potential without these explicit instructions, which these self-appointed motivational masters offer to you at a low, low price. The problem is, these people are all selling *different* success strategies. What do these karaoke academics have in common? They want you to believe that, if you follow their methods (and buy their products), they will give you the secret to unlimited motivation. Of course, few of these methods or products have much, if any, scientific basis.

Motivational speakers, authors, and aspiring YouTube entrepreneurs aren't the only people trying to convince others to follow their magical motivational rules. When children begin school, teachers tell them, "Everyone is required to follow the school rules." This approach to discipline is an attempt (a bad one!) to encourage students' motivation and to promote culturally accepted obedience behaviors. Company warlords do something similar; most organizations issue policy manuals and endorse a hierarchy of positions (cleverly disguised as an organizational chart), outlining who can supervise—and therefore supposedly lead and inspire. In each of these situations, people are operating under a false belief: that motivation can be learned from watching others, especially from anyone who has succeeded themselves. Each of these examples

frames the motivator as successful only when the "motivatee" passively relinquishes their motivational power. These behaviors are
the opposite of the *Anti-Power Hack,* which states when individuals
surrender their motivational control to others, they are unable to
reach their performance potential.

Why it works

People renounce their motivational power for several reasons. First,
it's easier. There is no need to engage in effortful Type 2 thinking
(p. 72) when you can just follow other people's instructions. Over
time, though, this makes passivity and compliance a habit. Being
willing to sacrifice this power also suggests certain beliefs about
the self and motivation: people who do this probably believe they
have minimal control (p. 114) over their lives (and will get better
outcomes if they listen to someone more knowledgeable), and they
probably also have little confidence in their own abilities. These
people are highly vulnerable to persuasion, and often believe the
key drivers of success are ability, relationships, or personality rather
than appropriate use of strategies and motivational techniques.

Second, many people are raised to believe that authority should
not be questioned. This encourages obedience when the person
offering advice knows more or has more experience or authority.
People with authority include parents, teachers, bosses, coaches,
and just about anyone wearing a uniform (yes, even security
guards—a uniform confers authority, legitimately or not). Third, people with certain dispositions are more likely to give up control. For
example, people who believe there is only one way to accomplish
a goal are quick to follow the advice of knowledgeable others, as
are people who strictly follow society's rules, whether or not those
rules are morally wrong. Last, people's need to be connected to
others underpins some control-relinquishing behavior. People who
don't feel like part of an in-group are extremely vulnerable to persuasion. This need is often the reason people are highly committed to
a specific ethnicity, race, religion, or political or social cause. When
we align with other like-minded thinkers, we satisfy our inherent
need to affiliate with others; we feel positive emotions, including

a sense of security, when we are surrounded by others that think, feel, behave like we do.

Application

To use the *Anti-Power Hack* effectively, you must recognize when you relinquish motivational power. As with other *Choice Hacks*, this means you must recognize which of your beliefs make you vulnerable to persuasion. Do you have an external locus of control? This belief makes you highly vulnerable to motivational influence, so you will benefit most from the *Anti-Power Hack*. Do you believe that intelligence is fixed or that it can be developed? If you believe suc- cess is capped (p. 93), when you reach the

YouTube video: *Anti-Power*

limit of your existing skills, you might turn to others and become subject to influence. If you unquestioningly follow advice because of the source rather than because of the quality of the advice, then the *Anti-Power Hack* is for you.

Level up the *Anti-Power Hack* by creating a judgment-free organizational culture. This trick is borrowed from current research into the best teaching practices, which put students at the center of decision-making. In these autonomous classrooms, rules and appropriate behaviors are not mandated by the teacher, but created through open discussion, with all stakeholders (professors and stu- dents) given equal voices in structuring the culture and the norms of desirable behavior. Organizations do something similar when they form self-directed work teams, which make decisions that would normally be made by company leadership. When people believe they can (p. 140) give input that will have real effects on their envi- ronments, they are much more willing to make suggestions and take risks, especially when the consequences of being wrong are small. Using the *Anti-Power Hack* does not require you to get rid of all rules and regulations. Instead, promote autonomy by emphasiz- ing creativity and diversity as key traits of an optimally functioning organization. When people know they are free to express their ideas without consequences or criticism, they are more likely to think independently and to refuse to turn over their thinking power and motivational growth to others.

18. Conformity Hack—*Don't mimic socially desirable behaviors at the expense of your individuality.*

The details

One thing I didn't tell you about the Fearsome Fivesome (p. 7) is that we liked to smoke—*anything*. We didn't care if it was weed, tobacco, or Bravos (lettuce leaves). If there was an opportunity to set something on fire and inhale, we did it. Back in the 1970s, if you wanted to be cool, you smoked. (If you wanted to be even cooler, you rolled your own tobacco in flavored rolling papers.) I never really enjoyed the taste or the feeling that resulted from smoking, but I did it anyway. Humans (all mammals, actually) imitate each other for the social satisfaction of fitting in. Try looking up at the sky in a large city, or dancing in a weird way with a partner, and you'll see this imitation in action: people will start copying your behavior. Social conformity is so powerful that we tend to like people who mimic our speech and gesture patterns. We are in love with imitation—one of the first games children play is Simon Says.

Acting like others isn't a problem as long as the imitated behavior is harmless. Trouble starts when we imitate deviant behavior: booing performers at stadiums, looting during riots, dancing Gangnam Style after 2012, or blindly following dictators and committing crimes against humanity. When we copy others, subconsciously we are neutralizing our own motivation—handing it off to others, adopting group motivation instead. We stop challenging flawed thinking and seem to give up our free will. If you need salient examples, just think of the Holocaust in Europe in the 1930s or slavery in colonial America. The *Conformity Hack* tells us that social conformity can destroy personal motivation. When we conform, we compromise our individuality; this compromise produces complacency, which limits what we can accomplish on our own.

Why it works

The *Conformity Hack* is extremely powerful because we *need* to exercise free will. Few people react positively to being told what to do or how to act. In fact, we are much more likely to work hard at the same task when we choose it than when we're told to complete it—our motivation is stronger when we resist the urge to conform. Conforming to others' behavior is like surrendering your motivational power (p. 117) to a karaoke academic: both decisions are a rejection of your own existing power (although for different reasons). When we conform, we unconsciously prioritize bonding over any other motive. We do this for good reasons; evidence from psychology and education consistently reveals that being excluded from a group inflicts social stress and pain. The biological reactions to social pain mirror those of physical harm—social rejection hurts in the same way that being cut or burned hurts. Conformity may be an attempt to satisfy biological, not psychological, needs.

Societal norms strongly influence conformity behavior around gender. When we behave according to expected gender norms, we are conforming to gender-normative behavior. If you aren't sure what I mean by gender-normative behavior, try wearing a dress to work if you identify as male, or construction boots and a necktie with your pants suit if you identify as female; you'll probably get a quick, sharp lesson in what others perceive as appropriate gender behavior. When we conform to expected gender roles, we are embraced and accepted by similar others in the culture, which feels good. But being part of the crowd has a downside. When we follow societal expectations to blend in, we lose motivational independence.

Application

The *Conformity Hack* is helpful when a situation needs individual or group creativity, such as academic group work, organizational brainstorming, or strategic planning. If we know when a person is

likely to succumb to others' social influence, we can work to counteract that tendency. For example, in a work group that is charged
with a task that requires creativity—developing policies, metrics,
or job descriptions, perhaps—some people may not want to offer
ideas because they don't want to seem weird. Those people are
more likely to speak up if there are incentives for doing so—offer
a reward for original ideas or for identifying potential flaws in the
group's decisions. This Hack is especially useful in classrooms,
where some learners don't engage because they fear classmates
will ridicule them (a form of social rejection) if they say something
questionable. Encouraging and rewarding diversity of opinion can
spark individual contributions. catalyze original ideas, and foster critical thinking.

Of course, conformity is based on cultural ideas about appropri-
ateness. When everyone wore JNCOs, you probably did too, *if* you
identified with the rave kids. As with many other Hacks, judgment
should be suspended (p. 128). Social conformity is neither good
nor bad; as a seasoned motivational hacker, you know by now that
motives change all the time. You are trying to understand why people behave the way they do, not judge them for it.

19. Social Identity Hack—*Bonding with others is a compelling motive.*

The details

Now I shall embarrass my daughter for the sake of giving you an
example of motivated behavior. Rebecca thrives on being with
friends. As a young child, she secretly arranged play dates with
half the neighborhood, often to the chagrin of her parents, who
only realized her machinations when a random child knocked on the
door. At eight years old, Rebecca, who had little interest in sports,
took up competitive roller-skating because her friends Alexandria
and Brooke did it. At fourteen, she snubbed bacon and become a
staunch vegetarian like her friend Emily. Rebecca's sociability runs

deep—it even influenced her career choice. She is a wedding planner, immersing herself in other people's social agendas. Her career decision is hardly a surprise, considering that she has exhibited this pronounced social motivation since birth.

Unlike people who situationally exhibit group conformity to fit in with a crowd, Rebecca's dominant motivation is relational. Many of her decisions and behaviors are influenced by the promise of socialization and by her anticipation that social interactions will be positive. Rebecca's self-concept—how she feels about herself and evaluates herself—is determined by her alignment with others. Socialization is a part of her identity. The *Social Identity Hack* emphasizes how much human relationships influence our behavior. If we were trying to help Rebecca succeed or to feel

YouTube video: Social Identity

valued, we would ensure that she could work with others; I can almost guarantee that she would thrive and have feelings of pride, inspiration, and accomplishment, and these positive emotions would stimulate her task interest and engagement, even if she was not especially in love with a particular task (like roller-skating).

Rebecca is not unique in tethering her task motivation to building relationships. Everyone considers social success at least a part of their overall self-evaluation. The *Social Identity Hack* makes us aware that relations with other people influence behavior and motivation. Figuring out how a person gains satisfaction and what guides their self-assessments helps you understand their motivations, which can predict future behavior.

Why it works

We form our identities through our lived experiences. We don't always know at the time which events and people are game changers, but we do know that we form beliefs about the self based on feedback from and experience with others. Our self-beliefs develop positively when we affiliate ourselves with people and groups who share our values: family, friends, people with similar backgrounds (religious, political, or ethnic), and people with similar interests (work

One of Italy's finest culinary contributions

or leisure). I happen to align with pizza eaters, cyclists, and those who are willing to share experiences I can write about. Regardless of group makeup, inclusion provides a sense of comfort and belonging and serves as a benchmark for aligning and grading our own behavior. Group affiliation can also serve as a barometer of perceived success, and our perception of how we fit into the group we choose drives our overall self-concept.

We don't incorporate all of our experiences into our identities, of course. Some people and some life events don't make the cut—they are incidental to how we view ourselves. While I enjoy eating pizza, it's not part of my identity. I don't resent burger-eaters. I don't join pizza-eating clubs so I can find other pizza devotees. I don't need pizza to feel positive about myself. For others, making and eating pizza are a vibrant part of their overall heritage, culture, and daily life. In psychological terms, people who open pizza parlors or travel the globe in a quest for the perfect slice have integrated pizza as part of their self-motivation and their identity. They do not need any incentive to pursue their mozzarella madness. For some, pizza is life, sufficient to satisfy needs, drive behavior, and define identity.

Application

There are far fewer people motivated by pizza than by a sense of kinship and belonging. As in many of the other *Choice Hacks*, if we take advantage of the *Social Identity Hack*, we can recognize when someone has internalized a certain quality or trait as part of their identity; we can then put them into the right situations and use the right strategies to develop their motivation. There are two main ways to use our knowledge of social motivation. First, recognize that all tasks are not equal. People hate tasks they think are boring, but for people who are motivated by social interaction, we can make even boring tasks bearable by making them social. This strategy is especially helpful for people who normally are motivated by avoidance—like teenagers. You may recall that I went to college purely to keep my mother off my back. But once I made some friends, I became more motivated to attend classes (although my academic engagement remained questionable).

Social motivation may also have unintended consequences. It may be situational, creating only a temporary interest in the actual activity or task. How long do you think Rebecca's quest for roller-skating superiority lasted? If you guessed "not long," you're right—her interest was fleeting, because skating was not part of her identity. Don't use social motivation as your only motivational tool, because it can produce shallow engagement and minimal commitment. Create situations that capitalize on *all* the existing strengths of your people. If you have a Rebecca on your team—someone who is motivated by establishing close relationships with others—by all means, let them leverage their interests and abilities. By setting others up to succeed, you create feelings of positive well-being for yourself and your whole team.

●

20. Interest Hack—*Use the power of interest to focus attention, influence choice, and promote engagement.*

The details

For as long as I can remember, magic tricks have fascinated me, although I am mediocre at prestidigitation, I can't saw women in half or levitate bodies, and I do not own a top hat or a rabbit. I never really had a clue about why I like magic. Then I remembered that when I was very young my grandfather often did some sleight of hand on our weekly visits. I vividly remember Grandpa Herman pulling things out of thin air, or from behind my ear, or out of my jacket pocket—usually, it was a tiny rectangular paper box with two pieces of Chiclets chewing gum inside. I also dredged up a memory of him showing me some brass contraption that turned a pile of nickels into dimes. Thinking about these memories, I realized that as a young child, my visits to my grandfather were always the highlight of my week, and that I associated warm feelings of family and togetherness with the childish magic tricks of my "Pa."

Interest explains why some of us love vegetables but others don't, why our favorite color is blue, not green, why we adore dogs but despise cats, and even (most importantly) why we favor certain people, tasks, and challenges over others. Interest, a combination of personal preferences and emotions, drives the activities we choose and how engaged (and re-engaged) we become in particular tasks. Interest begins when something in our environment triggers curiosity, and it can be fleeting or enduring, depending on how much attention we are willing to devote to it. Perhaps most importantly, interest sparks motivation to achieve. Although the precise value varies by person and task, interest typically accounts for about 15 percent of the difference in performance outcomes. In other words, the more interest we have in a task, the more likely we are to complete the task successfully, and with better results.

Why it works

Have you ever noticed that you read faster and comprehend more when you are interested in a topic than when you are not? Have you realized that when you are highly interested in a book, movie, or another person, time seems to pass more quickly? Clearly, greater interest enhances cognitive focus and intrusions are less likely to disrupt your concentration (p. 102). But how does interest develop in the first place? Interest begins with curiosity, which is triggered by something novel, surprising, or potentially useful. Interest persists beyond temporary inquisitiveness when whatever we are interested in is relevant and can potentially help us progress toward our long-term goals. Interest is also a function of confidence; when interest develops in a school or work task, it is usually because we believe we have the skills and ability to complete the task successfully. When we are confident, we invest more effort into the task and are more likely to stay engaged until the task is complete.

For interest to endure, we must perceive the task or activity as benefiting us in some way—enhancing our knowledge or well-being. When we perceive benefits, we have positive feelings while we are engaged in the task, and these upbeat feelings can help us persist even when the task becomes effortful and temporarily unfulfilling. The perception that we are getting smarter, faster, or more efficient also propels us forward. If we feel good and think we are learning something, we are likely to continue to work toward our target even when our energy is low or when we are juggling competing interests. You may recognize this phenomenon in your own life; perhaps you have deferred a bathroom break to finish an interesting task, or continued to work through being hungry or tired. The litmus test for enduring interest is the willingness to devote time and effort to a process that is not required or that doesn't offer a material reward.

Application

To use the *Interest Hack*, generate positive feelings about tasks or situations whose need, importance, or value may be in doubt. Developing interest is similar to persuading someone to change their beliefs: the person should see a compelling reason to change, should believe that engaging in the new activity will benefit them, and should feel that their success will be socially recognized. To increase interest, emphasize that interest drives success—it influences academic majors, college completion rates, and career choices.

The first step in promoting interest is making the experience emotionally satisfying. Orchestrate the environment to associate the interest target with positive feelings (happiness, gratification, pride, joy, excitement, and love). Consider providing an incentive for the person to engage. Incentives can be emotional (positive feedback, recognition for achievement) or material (money, opportunities). But *never* offer incentives when moderate task interest already exists; rewards diminish long-term interest, and removing incentives after interest is generated can lead to total disengagement. Third, the person should perceive the task as valuable, because they will evaluate themselves positively when they succeed. Finally, support the interest-acquiring person while their interest develops: model expert performance, provide feedback, and offer positive recognition about their developing skill or talent.

21. Beholder Hack—*Do not belittle self-motives or the motives of others. All motives are of similar importance to the person who is motivated by them.*

The details

I know a middle-aged fellow I'll call Jerry. Like many of us, Jerry goes to work dressed in clean clothes to support his family. On the weekend, he relaxes in his favorite worn-out sweatshirt and sweatpants, even if they haven't been washed since the previous weekend. Jerry refuses to spend any of his free time doing tedious chores like laundry, cleaning the house, or paying the bills. Jerry's son, Dylan, rather enjoys doing laundry because it calms his nerves and provides a sense of accomplishment. Dylan also believes that appearance is important, because people evaluate others based on first impressions, including appearance. Jerry, however, couldn't care less about his dowdy, unkempt appearance or what other people think. Dylan and Jerry deeply disagree about buying a new washing machine. The current one sounds like a lawnmower and often smells like a sewer. Jerry doesn't want to waste money on a new washer when the current one is (in his opinion) sufficient. Dylan, who believes cleanliness is next to godliness, demands a new machine. Who is right?

Jerry and Dylan have different washing machine beliefs. For now, let's assume both Jerry and Dylan have valid laundry opinions and that neither is right about the value of appearance. We assign value to categories based on our personal experiences, on cultural influences, and on how we think. Some people are taught from birth that there are huge differences between right and wrong. Inflexible people rarely change their opinions and tend to blindly follow directions from trusted authorities. *Relativist* types believe that everyone is entitled to their own opinion and that all opinions are equally valid, meaning that there is no absolute right or wrong. These people frequently say things like, "I understand what you are saying, so let's agree to disagree." A third type of thinker believes that there is a perfect solution to every problem; the *idealist* thinker operates under the premise that who is "right" changes based on the situation and who is involved. According to the *Beholder Hack*, if we can accurately determine someone's thinking style (which varies according to the issue), we can predict how they will behave when faced with a similar problem.

Why it works
The *Beholder Hack* implies that motivational intensity is influenced by our thinking beliefs. I don't mean that one approach produces more motivated people than another; I mean that identifying thinking style can help explain behavior. Jerry and Dylan are both highly inflexible and resistant thinkers, although they have different

cleanliness and laundry beliefs. People who share the same thinking style can have opposite opinions. The decision someone makes
is not necessarily the most revealing thing about their behavior;
understanding *why* the decision was made tells us more about
underlying motives than merely knowing a person's position on an
issue.

To improve how well we predict other people's motivations, we
should pay attention to the mysterious factors that psychologists call

epistemological beliefs— beliefs about how we
acquire knowledge and how sure we are about
what we know. These beliefs affect how we navigate the world. When we think it will be complicated or effortful to acquire knowledge, we may
decide it's too much trouble to really examine
what is right or wrong and default to positions

YouTube video:
Beholder

that do not require effortful thinking—believing
someone else's account of a situation, for example, or deciding
(based on emotional Type 1 thinking) that whoever is most like-
able is right. Clearly, cultural differences factor into decisions about
right and wrong: they shape how we think people should respond
to others and what we consider appropriate behavior. But thinking
style plays an enormous role. An inflexible thinker, who strongly
believes that there is only one right way to approach a problem, will
be unlikely to consider alternative solutions unless they come from
a respected authority; a relativist thinker is more likely to consider
other perspectives if they offer a convincing argument; and the idealist thinker, who is committed to finding an overall best solution,
will carefully weigh each option before reaching a decision.

Application

The *Beholder Hack* is useful in many persuasion situations, and it
can also be particularly helpful when people should start thinking
about new approaches to a task. For example, students who are
struggling to master course material might benefit from a different
approach to studying. I know many students who insist on listening
to background music while studying, even though listening to music

hijacks attentional and cognitive resources that otherwise would be devoted to studying. Parents or teachers will find it difficult to convince the student to kill the music. But if the student is a relativist thinker or if they highly value academic performance, then offering them strong evidence about successful study strategies could get them to unplug the headphones.

This works for organizational decisions too. Company executives sometimes make decisions based on intuitive or emotional factors without considering all the available evidence. Although these decisions are usually implemented unilaterally, knowing the boss's thinking style can help you influence what happens after the decision is made. Once, I needed to convince the dean of my college that changing the admission requirements for one degree program would impact the number of applications that other programs received. Because I knew that our dean always evaluates the impact of her decisions on everyone, I pointed out that her decision could give the impression of favoring one program over another. When presented with this additional evidence, she reversed her original decision. To maximize the benefit of the *Beholder Hack*, use your assessment of the person's thinking style to develop a customized response.

22.Target Hack—*Create one goal to relentlessly pursue. Literally keep the goal in your visual field.*

The details
Many students new to my courses believe in multitasking, but the scientific evidence says we can't allocate mental resources to different tasks at the same time. I quickly dispel the myth of multitasking in my classes: I challenge a student to write the alphabet while simultaneously reciting their ABC's using a normal speaking pace. The results are usually hilarious—the speaking part sounds like an Ariana Grande video played at half-speed. But despite the research, many of us believe that we can simultaneously pursue multiple

high-level goals without any compromise in the quality or efficiency of the outcomes. If you think you can do your best work without giving it your full attention and effort, you are fooling yourself.

The *Target Hack* tells us to choose one goal at a time—the one that is most important to our overall well-being. Once we choose the goal, we should create optimal conditions for reaching the goal and deliberately implement strategies that will accelerate goal attainment. One example of this type of *Target Hack* goal is the career plan designed by my friend Genna. At only twenty-one, Genna's dreams are crystal clear and in Technicolor. She wants to be a successful, independent woman who travels the world at her leisure, sharing her experiences through her photography and through blogging. Genna structures her behaviors around attaining this goal; she devotes her time to learning new languages, trying exotic cuisine, and actively seeking a diverse group of friends that can expose her to different cultures. In fact, I initially met Genna during a study-abroad language program in Florence, Italy. Her coordinated approach doesn't mean she avoids other activities or shuns people who can't help her reach her objective. Genna simply has a well-thought-out plan that includes definable, measurable steps that bring her closer to her goal each day. Clearly, Genna refuses to compromise her goal when obstacles crop up; she knows what makes her happy.

Why it works

We all want to improve ourselves—what we think of as improvement is, of course, highly subjective. Our notion of improvement is primarily based on how much we value an outcome and what upgrade benefits we expect. The more value we ascribe to a goal, the more effort we are willing to invest to achieve it. But there is a gap between wanting and getting. Even if we had unlimited motivation, trying to reach several goals at the same time—splitting our effort—would almost certainly mean we would come up short. I mean, if I told you to memorize a fifteen-digit number in ten seconds while also listening to instructions about how to build a house, you probably couldn't recall both things accurately. You can't give your full attention and total effort toward several different things at once—the brain has limited processing capacity, and no matter how smart you are, you must be selective about where and how you apply these limited resources. Instructional designers work with these processing limitations when designing learning materials; they work to avoid "split attention," which happens when a picture or chart is on one page and the text that goes with it is somewhere else. When we shift our attention back and forth between the image and the text, it creates cognitive overload, and learning suffers. The same thing happens when we spread our finite motivational resources too thin with multiple goals.

There is one more thing to think about when you are setting goals. Some of us set up aggressive goals that are almost impossible to reach. Why do we do this? It's a psychological attempt to protect our egos. If we don't succeed, we can blame our failure on the ridiculousness of the goal. This protects us from questioning our own abilities—if only Captain America or Wonder Woman could possibly reach a difficult goal, then it's no failure for us to fall short. This is usually called self-handicapping, but it's nothing more than taking out an ego insurance policy that pays off huge in self-esteem dollars when disaster happens.

Application
The *Target Hack* has many practical applications: it can help you start a business, earn a technical certification or degree, find a life partner—really, it can help you reach any specific, measurable outcome you choose. Whatever you want to accomplish, the Hack helps you actively block out distractions that might interfere with achieving your goal. Intrusions will invariably pop up, but having a plan that anticipates problems will keep you on target to reach your goal. The key is making *daily* progress and never taking your eyes off the target.

You can be like Genna and coordinate your life around your dreams, or you can try the very simple strategy that my entrepreneurial friend Robert Knowling used as a teenager. When Robert was young, he shared a bedroom with his older brother, who slept in the bottom bunk of their bunk beds. After plenty of convincing, Robert persuaded his brother to switch beds with him. Robert developed his primary goal early in life: to start a landscaping business (he accomplished this goal when he was eleven). As a constant reminder, he wrote his goal on a piece of paper and taped it to the underside of the top bunk so he could stare at his goal every night before he went to sleep. Robert was implementing the *Target Hack*. Once he knew what he wanted, he used a concrete visual reminder to maintain his focus. Although Robert merely wrote his goal, you can keep your top priority in mind using any symbol that visually represents the goal and reminds you to focus on achieving it: a picture of a loved one, a calendar with a deadline circled, a dollar bill, a slogan, even a Chinese fortune cookie message taped to your monitor. Just visualize the outcome—never take your eyes or mind off your target.

23. Competence Hack—*By knowing how people define competence, you can reliably predict their behavior and socialization.*

Dr. Feenstra

Athletic, mature, and outgoing. Likes to eat sprinkle-encrusted ice cubes and take long walks in the forest foraging mushrooms. Has expert knowledge of ceramic gnomes and an award-winning stuffed caterpillar collection. Globally recognized for lime Jell-O recipes and Speedo beachwear. Seeks similar individual for competitive eating contests and Kardashian marathons.

The details

Personal ads are fun to read, but do the ads reveal anything useful—can they tell us what makes the writer jump out of bed in the morning? Probably not. The ads provide biased, self-reported information about a person, and we all tell people what we think they want to hear; some of us either don't realize what makes us tick or can't effectively communicate our motives. Authentic or not, self-descriptions do give information about how we want others to perceive us. We all share a desire to be seen as competent, for instance, and this motivation often determines what we do, where we do it, and who we do it for. When we understand how a person defines competence, we can more accurately predict how they will behave, especially around other people.

The *Competence Hack* takes advantage of the fact that each of us has particular things that make us feel valued and important. Value is self-determined; it is based on a combination of self-perception and how we think are seen and judged by others. When we assess our competence, we look at our dominant attributes—the qualities that define us as individuals. Many different qualities can contribute to a sense of competence, but everyone knows what makes them feel competent. For example, in a recent class discussion of competence, my students asked me how I evaluate my own competence. I said that having broad motivational knowledge was an important competence for me, since I am an educational psychology professor, but that to feel competent in all areas of my life, I also live a healthy lifestyle, try to treat all people with kindness, spend time with the people I care about, and work to increase other people's happiness through generosity or effort. Remember the *Beholder Hack* (p. 128); my definition of competence is not better than yours, just different. When we know which traits, values, and beliefs we hold and other people hold, we can better understand motives and predict behavior.

Why it works

We all need to feel competent. Getting that feeling is a primary motivation; when we feel competent, we are energized by our assessments of our abilities. To feel competent, we must believe that we have what it takes to be successful. A feeling of competence also increases social confidence; we feel comfortable with other people when we feel competent, and incompetence produces social distance, feelings of awkwardness, and general apathy—we are reluctant to expose our weaknesses to the world.

When we feel competent—when we believe that we can orchestrate change in our lives, and when we see how our efforts affect the people around us—it motivates us. For example, if

YouTube video:
Competence

my Facebook post gets a thousand likes, I will believe I have made a meaningful contribution to my community of friends and that I am valued. After repeated similar instances, I integrate these perceptions of value into my overall sense of self: I am valuable. Competence is not only derived from tasks; we incorporate values, beliefs, and even dispositions into our self-definitions. You probably know some people who pride themselves on being pleasant, agreeable, and sociable, and others who want to be seen as grumpy, contrarian, or radical. Regardless of how people satisfy the competence motive, it drives behavior as people seek to reinforce positive self-perceptions and avoid negative self-attributions.

Application

The ultimate purpose of the *Competence Hack* is to predict future behavior, especially behavior around self-improvement. Someone whose self-perceptions focus on knowledge-building will probably describe him- or herself as a "lifelong learner" and do things that promote education (like my plunge into full-time graduate school [p. 41] at age forty-six), including leisure activities that support intellectual growth (Scrabble, Sudoku, reading, watching documentaries). The *Competence Hack* can also help us predict what people value, which gives us information about what they are motivated to do: people universally try to avoid tasks they perceive as low-value (the atheist doesn't spend Sunday mornings at church, and the person who doesn't see themselves as athletic doesn't play competitive sports). Don't forget that the socialization needs may supersede any other primary need, including competence. Remember that Rebecca took up competitive roller-skating (p. 122) primarily to satisfy her need to connect with friends.

24. Internalization Hack—*The best performances are achieved when professional goals become part of your personal identity.*

The details

If you overheard people talking about you at a party, would their descriptions of you match your own self-descriptions? To accurately describe you, they would have to know what is important to you—what values, activities, behaviors, and beliefs you hold as part of your sense of self. The *Internalization Hack* tells us that people *internalize*, or make part of their self-concept, the things that are most important to them. When my last book was published, I was interviewed by a blogger named Abby with a strong and distinctive personality. As we talked, I realized she was a nonconformist who wanted to be seen as rebellious and unorthodox. Abby refused to support societal rules she disagreed with, such as imprisoning people for minor drug offenses. She said she would never work in a traditional job, and that lawyers, law enforcement personnel, and corporate executives are despicable creatures preying on common citizens for profit. She was adamantly pro-environmental protection and believed that climate change is the world's greatest challenge. There could be no misunderstanding what Abby valued and considered important; her job, personality, and identity aligned almost perfectly.

Abby embodies her values—in fact, she rejected a traditional career in social work to become an entrepreneur and promote her causes in a variety of different ways. She spends much of her free time writing, interviewing people with similar values who write books and give speeches about their beliefs. She is highly active on social media, trying to influence others to align with her and challenge the status quo. Perhaps most interestingly, Abby volunteers her time; she makes little, if any, money from all this. Nothing is more important to her than staying true to her beliefs. On more than one occasion she has ended friendships with people who disagreed with her views. Abby is a model example of someone who has taken the *Internalization Hack* to its limits; she has internalized her beliefs and values so strongly that her identity cannot be separated from them.

Why it works

The *Internalization Hack* can help you understand how people's behavior represents their personal identities. Like the *Competence Hack* (p. 134), the *Internalization Hack* is based on the premise that humans have basic needs that must be satisfied for us to feel content. We need to achieve competence, as discussed in the *Competence Hack* section; we also need to believe we have choices and that we can exercise our agency to move toward our goals in the way that we think is best. The *Internalization Hack* suggests people will not need external incentives—money, recognition, or praise—to wholeheartedly invest effort toward completing some tasks. Sometimes people do things just because they love them. If we know what is motivating someone to complete a task and how much they have internalized that task as a part of their identity, we can also calculate how committed they are to the task.

Sometimes we decide to do things—usually fun things—purely voluntarily: perhaps we expect a pleasurable experience, or maybe we have an enduring interest (p. 126) in the task. Other times we feel obligated to do the things we do; this is how most of us feel about school or work tasks. But there are some people who voluntarily engage in tasks that require hard work and intentional learning, because they genuinely enjoy exerting effort and value the act of learning. For these people, hard work *is* fun. They want to learn and grow, not rake in cash hand over fist at a job they don't enjoy or collect a status-symbol diploma from an impressive-sounding university. These people don't need a payoff other than the intrinsic rewards provided by the activity itself. This is not to say that people who work hard never care about getting a paycheck or pats on the back from friends and family for accomplishments—just that these incentives are secondary. How do we explain why some people happily dive headfirst into cognitively demanding, effortful activities like work and school? These people have internalized working and learning as part of their identities—they *are* workers and learners. People who (like Abby) are satisfied by accomplishment itself are said to be intrinsically motivated. Doing what is important to them is enough to fulfill their needs; they don't need incentives to do hard things that many of us do only out of obligation. The more the task and the values it represents are internalized, the less people need external incentives. If you can determine how deeply someone has internalized particular tasks, you can use this powerful tool to help you diagnose their motives.

Application

Task internalization gives you helpful information when you are choosing a team, deciding whether to volunteer for something, or predicting whether someone will follow through on a commitment. Remember that internalization fluctuates between tasks: the person who needs no incentive to read a book on astrology might need significant persuasion to read a statistics textbook. And be cautious; some people may seem to have internalized a task, but in reality may be acting only out of guilt or obligation to please someone else. Their behavior may look like task engagement based on internalization, but their motives for engagement might not match their behavior. People can give an impression of enthusiasm while merely going through the motions.

Although internalization operates on a continuum, the commitment itself is relatively fixed. If someone has truly incorporated a task or activity into their personal identity, their commitment does not waver when conditions related to the task change. In other words, internalization is enduring, and changes in difficulty or momentary lapses in motivation should not influence task success. The greater the internalization, the greater the commitment, the more energy and effort will be invested, and the higher the likelihood the task will be performed to completion. While it's hard to know for sure if some-one has internalized a task, observing what people do during their free time can provide clues. For example, many people struggle to maintain an exercise regimen. If you had no external pressure from loved ones, weren't subject to social comparison, and encountered no media messages about the importance of fitness, would you still exercise? If your answer is yes, you have internalized fitness as part of your identity. If not, mind your health!

25. Option Hack—*To enhance motivation, create choices.*

The details

Let's face it: the typical North American does not like to be told what to do. One of the founding documents of the United States is the Declaration of Independence, which asserts our inalienable right to freedom; we often complain about following arbitrary rules and regulations passed by bureaucrats. Parents, teachers, and leaders are reminded to empower their children, students, and employees by offering them real, viable choices that actually affect outcomes. This is the basis of the *Option Hack*, which I frequently use with my own students to beef up their academic enthusiasm. Most of my classes require a presentation; students can choose to present live in class or to moderate an online discussion. Students choose their own presentation topics and how they will demonstrate their mas-tery in the course project. While I maintain control of how projects are evaluated, students have full control over content.

Offering choices gives people the sense that they control when and how they invest their energy. Choice facilitates commit-ment; after choosing an option, people look for reasons that justify their choice as the correct one. We can learn a lot about people's motives by observing their behavior around choice. For example, once someone makes a choice, it would be strange for them to make only halfhearted efforts toward reaching their chosen goal. If you observe someone just going through the motions, it probably means that all the choice options seemed low-value. Of course, enthusiasm for a task can wax and wane as the task progresses, but any change in behavior gives us additional information. Most importantly, choice variability shows diversity of interests. In other words, given the same set of choices, people choose differently: what is satisfying and invigorating to one person may be boring and awful to another. Ultimately, conscious choices are robust indicators of individual commitment and give us important information about how people value various outcomes.

Why it works

Exercising choice is a demonstration of free will. It shows that you can express and achieve your desires. Choice may be restricted by environmental factors such as cultural norms, government control, or organizational policy, and expectations of autonomy are clearly influenced by individual beliefs: even under iden-tical conditions, two people exhibiting the same behavior will have different perceptions of con-trol. For example, in cultures where arranged marriage is commonplace, the participants in arranged marriages may not feel a lack of con-trol; however, in individualistic cultures like North America, where arranged marriage is rejected,

YouTube video:
Option

participants would likely feel they lack control. Choice behavior is highly influenced by the social and cultural environment; people conform to stay in good standing with the group and to feel good about themselves for fitting in.

Free choice often produces anxiety or doubt about whether the right choice was made. When people choose among various options (as when choosing what brand to buy), they retroactively seek evidence to shore up their decision. For example, once we decided upon the title of *Hack Your Motivation*, Dr. Feenstra and I assured each other that no other title could be as appealing. In other words, people have a strong desire to eliminate what psychologists call *cognitive dissonance*—two or more simultaneously held, contradictory thoughts. In the case of choice, cognitive dissonance comes from thinking you made a good choice (or you wouldn't have chosen it) and at the same time worrying that you chose the wrong option. When we reaffirm to ourselves we made the right choice, we quell this psychological discomfort and feel good about our decisions. When people don't feel they have choices, the *Option Hack* is useless—forced choices often create avoidance rather than motivation or positive emotion. And before using the Hack, think about the consequences of choosing the wrong option. In relationships and job decisions, people often stay in unhappy situations for too long, in part because once the choice is made, it feels immutable—they have internalized the choice and feel obligated to stick with it. A long series of failed choices may lead to choice reluctance, rendering the person indecisive and willing to accept the status quo because they fear making yet another poor decision.

Application

The *Option Hack* is especially helpful in cultivating enthusiasm about choices. Using the Hack doesn't guarantee that students, loved ones, or coworkers will jump around like lottery winners as they choose between broccoli and spinach, or between research papers and group presentations. But choice always trumps force, and people are more likely to be enthusiastic about an option they have chosen. Classrooms are ripe environments for the *Option Hack*; offering choices reduces the perception of teacher control and gives learners a voice in their classroom. The Hack is also ideal for workplaces where employees work in teams; teams reduce emphasis on hierarchies and power structures and promote choice. In both classrooms and workplaces, integrating choice with opportunities for socialization fosters enthusiasm.

The *Option Hack* works best when people are given tactical, rather than strategic, flexibility. Tactical flexibility means that the teacher, boss, or parent drafts parameters for acceptable choices rather than giving free rein over all aspects of a decision. For example, if your family is planning a vacation, don't offer the kids an open-ended invitation to decide where you'll go and what you'll do; they are likely to choose places and activities you can't afford or don't have time for. Instead, offer a set of acceptable potential options that will appeal to your family, and emphasize their autonomy in choosing among the options. If an option they want isn't possible, provide a reasonable explanation and empathize with their frustration. Ultimately, in workplaces, families, and learning environments, supporting autonomy improves performance.

26. Club Hack—*Who you align with reveals your values.*

The details

In the mid-1960s, when nine-year-old latchkey me (p. 11) got home from elementary school, my activity of choice was watching television reruns of *The Three Stooges Show*, *Superman*, or B-grade horror movies like The Incredible Shrinking Man. As I did my homework, the lyrics from one of the most popular children's television shows of the era would blare in the background. The show, *The Mickey Mouse Club*, had celebrities on every week to sing along with the lucky kids in the cast. Don't be too envious, though—metaphorically speaking, we are all in a club. As adults, our clubs don't worship fictional rodents through song; they are alliances grounded in a common set of values and behaviors shaped by ethnicity, politics, religion, work, musical preferences, even spending patterns. Commonalities—similar attributes or comparable beliefs—bond people together.

In this book, being in a club doesn't mean going to meetings or participating in an initiation or getting hazed. The *Club Hack* is a way to figure out how people satisfy their psychological need to connect with other people. The clubs you join reveal who you choose to affiliate with and under what circumstances. Clubs can be partnerships between individuals, as in romantic relationships, but this need to affiliate can also be met through relationships with people at work or school, or even by affiliating with a spiritual being and with other worshipers. Affiliation needs can even be met when people have negative life events or circumstances in common—after all, misery loves company. Knowing which club(s) someone joins gives us valuable evidence about their values and how they like to connect with others.

Why it works

We need to be close with other people and to feel valued, and this need can motivate superior performance. When a person's affiliation need is satisfied, they have positive feelings because they feel valued by other members of the club. The relationship among group members metaphorically "fences in" member behavior; norms of the group determine which member behaviors are acceptable and which actions will be rewarded by the group. The affiliation motivation is nearly a biological need. Research across disciplines shows that people who are connected to others get sick less often, recover more quickly from illness, and evaluate their well-being more positively than those whose affiliation need is unfulfilled. Emotional connections with others develop through sharing common experiences in the context of a strong, durable relationship. Strong emotional connections serve as a mutual validation of respect and recognition, generating positive self-views that reinforce personal values and sense of personal worth.

Organizationally, when people feel related, they respect and rely on each other more. Work cultures that emphasize teamwork and foster cohesiveness have lower employee turnover, fewer company layoffs, and more profitable operations. Group participation can, on its own, enhance task interest; this is especially valuable for boring or repetitive tasks. Parents, teachers, and leaders should use the *Club Hack* by creating group activities and teams to leverage the social nature of productivity. Group work's social conditions foster loyalty among group members and solidify bonds of trust as they rely on each other for support. Synergistic benefits from close working relationships include reacting more positively to supervision, greater willingness to help coworkers, and lower levels of workplace favoritism.

Application

The *Club Hack* can be used at the individual and the group level. Individually, many people maximize their productivity when their affiliation needs are fulfilled. Although some people who perceive themselves as loners or introverts may not believe it, when affiliation needs are properly met, even the most reclusive person can become a social butterfly. The need for socialization and alignment with others can be a primary motivation to participate (p. 122); people are often reluctant to take on challenging tasks alone. To satisfy affiliation needs, people tend to look for others like themselves, but leaders should strive to help diverse people affiliate, because this will help all team members develop. Watch out though—too much collegiality can impair performance if group members focus more on socialization than on task progress. Objectively evaluate each situation to ensure that the need for affiliation is balanced with the individual productive output of group members.

Group cohesiveness is a hallmark of a productive and profitable organization. When group members are aligned, they perform well. Cohesive work groups encourage agreeableness and conscientiousness among group members, and this produces solid, trusting relationships. There is a strong relationship between team cohesiveness and positive workplace behaviors: strong teams are more likely to successfully complete projects, more willing to agree with other team members, more in control of their personal impulses, and more helpful. Organizations can leverage the power of the *Club Hack* by creating incentives that encourage members to socialize. Some organizations may see work-related social programs as burdensome, but the intangible socialization benefits outweigh the direct costs. When employees feel comfortable in their work environment, engagement increases and productivity soars.

●

27. Mask Hack—*Gaps exist between who you are and who you want to be. Some people disguise the gap to feel better about themselves.*

The details

The drill plunged into Rick's head, instantly shattering his skull. Rita crashed into the wall and felt mortified; she swore she would never go ice skating again. Rick and Rita both experienced pain, a subjective feeling that can be based in either physical or emotional harm. Physicians diagnosing severe injuries routinely ask patients to evaluate pain on a scale from one to ten, but can the pain from burns or cuts be compared to the pain from embarrassment, shame, and humiliation? Surprisingly, the body makes little neurological distinction between physical and psychological pain, reacting with the same hormones and neurotransmitters to both types. While physicians blunt physical discomfort with prescriptions, mental and emotional pain are often left untreated—diagnosed only by the experiencer. This is, in part, because emotional pain is less visible to untrained observers than physical pain; it may also be because, in many cultures, acknowledging emotional pain is often perceived as weakness.

Left untreated, pain from psychological stress may disrupt routine behaviors as the person strives to eliminate the source of their discomfort and anxiety. Some people, like ice-skating Rita, avoid certain people, situations, or contexts to reduce their pain. Other people may choose more destructive strategies to ease their psychological pain. To deflect self-doubt, people may engage in excessive drinking, eating, or sex; others may abuse drugs, other people, or even their own bodies, intentionally harming themselves to redirect emotional pain to a more acceptable source. Nothing is more depressing and debilitating than realizing that you are someone you don't want to be.

Why it works

When people perceive a gap between their desired self and their actual self, they seek to close the gap. When people self-evaluate, they assess their current self-image and compare it to their ideal self-image. If the two are relatively close, people feel good about themselves (they experience high self-worth); if the two are quite far apart, they feel inadequate. These self-evaluations include evaluations of competence and capability—both generally and in the context of a particular task. The more a task is valued, the more likely it is that our competence and capability *at that task* will affect how we evaluate our self-worth. These tasks against which we measure our worth are called *behavioral anchors*, and they come in an enormous range. Some people focus on basic skill sets, and others may dwell on social status or living up to the expectations of valued others, such as parents or partners.

Self-worth gaps can be closed in at least three different ways. A psychologically healthy, or *adaptive*, approach is to address skills that need upgrading by taking measurable steps toward improvement. This gap-closing method requires the user to know that change is beneficial, to understand that they must work to improve their skill levels, and to be able to take and use constructive feedback. A second, less healthy approach is to buffer the pain of recognizing the skill gap through intentional avoidance or by masking the pain in socially destructive ways, as discussed earlier. I don't need to worry about my social awkwardness if I stay home watching television, or if I drink enough that I no longer care. Third, and most insidious, people use subtle redirection strategies that shift inadequacy from the self onto external circumstances. People who redirect might procrastinate, set unobtainable goals, or view a required, important task as low-value. These redirections insulate the user from self-blame when they (almost inevitably) fail. A procrastinator can convince themselves that procrastination, not low ability or limited effort, was at fault for bad performance. This blame-shifting keeps self-worth intact because the person believes that if they had not procrastinated, they would have succeeded.

Application
The *Mask Hack* is designed to determine whether people are using productive or nonproductive strategies to close perceived skill gaps. To use the *Mask Hack* on yourself, first objectively evaluate where you are, then take measurable steps to improve skills and abilities.

To use the *Mask Hack* with others, look for situational satisfaction, which offers clues about self-assessments. People evaluate their self-worth based on perceptions of ability; they gravitate toward environments and activities that foster positive self-assessments and avoid situations that may expose their personal vulnerabilities. If the person seems unsatisfied, determine whether they are using productive or maladaptive strategies to mediate the perceived gap. Masks come in all shapes and sizes, but each serves the same purpose: shielding the inner psyche from anxiety and reminders of inadequacy, whether real or imagined.

Once you know what type of strategy they are using, help the person look at the endgame of that strategy: is it success or failure? Ask questions like, "How do you feel when you are unsuccessful?" or "Tell me about a time when you used a different approach and accomplished your goal?" or "What is the potential downside to using your approach?" to help the person see whether their strategy is productive. If it is counterproductive, suggest other approaches that will produce better results (and may require less work). The key to successfully implementing the *Mask Hack* is to help the person realize that not all anxiety-reducing strategies are useful in the long run. To be considered successful, psychological gap-narrowing strategies must do more than just make the person feel better.

28. Helper Hack—*Knowing why people help others can predict social behavior.*

The details

Many of us associate holidays with giving gifts. Sometimes we give gifts to generate warm feelings in others. Sometimes we give gifts to show our appreciation for the valued people in our lives—the gift is a material symbol of the connection between the gift giver and the recipient. Sometimes we give gifts out of obligation (we all know that awkward feeling when someone unexpectedly gives us a gift and we don't have one for them). In these gift-giving scenarios, the same behavior comes from different motivations and confers different psychological benefits. We know that it is better to give than to receive, but what are the actual benefits of the act of giving?

Perhaps Larry Stewart, the Secret Santa of Kansas City, Missouri, can help us understand. Larry arbitrarily gave out hundred-dollar bills to people in need—people he found shivering at bus stops or waiting in line for assistance at social services agencies. Before Stewart died in 2007, he gave away more than a hundred thousand dollars to complete strangers without any tangible benefit to himself. Stewart's acts are an example of *altruism*, an expenditure of the self in service of others without expecting anything in return. But did Stewart's acts of kindness have *no* benefits for him? Obviously, Stewart's behavior was reported in the media, and so at the very least he earned positive reactions from other people. Stewart likely felt gratified by the public response, which elevated his own feelings, reinforcing his gifting behavior. After Stewart was diagnosed with cancer, he elected to tell his story to the press. He explained that his philanthropy was motivated by his own early poverty—he knew what it was like to struggle to survive without help. Stewart did good things, but whose needs was he really satisfying?

Why it works

We often give priority to the needs of others over our own: a diabetic might buy a box of Girl Scout cookies, or a young man, late for work, might help an elderly lady cross the street. Sometimes we want to feel good about ourselves, sometimes we genuinely want to reduce the distress of others, and sometimes we want to act on our social responsibility beliefs. These three highly divergent reasons for helping others all contribute to satisfying the basic human need for affiliation (p. 143) described earlier, and all are likely to make the helper feel good. But there is much more to explaining voluntary philanthropy.

When we help others succeed, we satisfy our innate need to create positive relationships. Cooperating with someone else raises both people's moods. There is no such thing as classic altruism, which delivers *no* benefits to the provider; even when we help

someone completely anonymously, we are reinforcing our competency beliefs (p. 134), boosting our personal egos, and raising our
perceptions of self-worth. It also feels good when people appreciate our actions, making us look good publicly—this is an especially powerful motivator for people who base their self-worth on
comparisons to others. While most research on helping looks at
altruism from a behavioral perspective (which assumes that we
only act to get rewards, whether explicit or implicit), we also know
that some people persist in giving time or money after they have
already received the gratitude and the back-pats. These people are
likely not motivated by ego benefits alone.

Application

The *Helper Hack* tells us that if we can decipher helping motives
either in the self or in others, we can cultivate helping behaviors.
Many people voluntarily work hard on tasks that seem to have no
reward, and learning why people choose to pursue these tasks

YouTube video:
Helper

can help us learn how to increase motivation
for other tasks. To encourage helping behavior,
set things up so helpers get their egos boosted.
Recognition is the normal reward for voluntary
service; volunteers are always being publicly
applauded for their dedicated service to others,
especially people who volunteer for civic duty or
the military, help disadvantaged children or the

elderly, or work in low-paying helping professions—first responders
or teachers. I thoroughly enjoy the 10 percent educator discount I
receive at the beef jerky store, offered in appreciation for my toil at
my public university teaching job. You can also encourage helping
behavior by creating opportunities for volunteers to build relationships. The prosocial motive alone—sometimes the only benefit to
helping—can make the difference between acceptance or rejection
of a helping request.

Organizationally, people usually volunteer because employers value it. Employers don't always value volunteerism in the
workplace, though; offering unsolicited help can seem insulting,

especially if it's not part of the contributor's job description. When people consider helping, they complete a (usually rapid, informal) cost-benefit analysis that considers the psychological and social benefits of offering help and the emotional costs if their offer is rejected. Companies can leverage the *Helper Hack* and satisfy altruism motives by creating supportive cultures where helping is the expectation, even when helping isn't explicitly part of a particular job description. When company leadership values prosocial behavior, employees are more likely to follow their lead. One key is creating a culture in which accepting help doesn't signal failure or skill deficiency—instead, it supports the organization's growth through individual development.

●

This chapter aimed to explain how and why individual beliefs influence our own and others' behavior. *Choice Hacks* examined the self-evaluations that precede motivated behavior. When choices are critically examined, you can better predict what tasks and activities a person will pursue, and better understand why people are more comfortable and confident in some situations than others. *Choice Hacks* are especially important because our choices define how we see ourselves in relation to the world, and our decisions reveal how we want others to see us—our public face. Now that you are aware of the many factors that influence choice, it is time to make some choices and act upon the decisions by using *Action Hacks,* which are the specific strategies and approaches you'll use to reach your goals and Hack Your Motivation.

CHAPTER FIVE

Action Hacks

BY NOW YOU UNDERSTAND how self-beliefs influence your decisions and how decisions drive motivated action. The next step in hacking your motivation is learning and implementing the strategies that will help you efficiently reach your goals. The *Action Hacks* in this chapter are tools for your motivational tool chest. Ask any carpenter—selecting and using the right tool for the job is part of doing the job well. Each strategy described here is useful, but knowing *which* approach to use and *when* to use it can make the difference between success and failure. Choose wisely. Don't try to kill a fly with a hammer. Study all the strategies *before* you take action.

29. Reality Hack—*Expect adversity, delays, and frustration. Plan ahead to move forward despite setbacks.*

The details

Does the following story sound familiar? You are flying cross-country and arranged things to travel as efficiently as possible. Your flight is scheduled to land at a convenient time for the friend you are visiting, who will pick you up at the airport during her lunch hour. You arrive at the airport two hours before your planned departure, but once you get through security and are settled at the gate, you discover that your flight will be delayed by an hour. Not a major setback, but annoying. As the hour passes, you become anxious—the friend who is picking you up has to be back at work after lunch, and if your flight arrives too late, you'll have to figure out alternative ground transportation. When you finally board the flight and get settled in your seat, the ominous loudspeaker clicks on: "Good morning, ladies and gentleman, this is Captain Earhart. We will not be departing the gate for another 45 minutes." Now what will you do?

There are several different reactions to this scenario. Some people become extremely agitated and show it with facial grimaces or exasperated sighs. Others vent to fellow passengers, exchanging tales of previous travel woes. Some people get restless; they probably can't use the extra time to get work done because their concentration is hampered by anxiety. People may frequently check the time or get annoyed with other passengers who don't seem fazed by the delay. But some travelers realize that delays are an inevitable part of the traveling process. These people may be unaffected because they prepared for the likelihood of inconvenience and planned to use any extra time productively—returning phone calls, answering emails, or reading a book. Planning ahead minimizes the disruption caused by delays, and in some cases, can even turn delay into a positive, allowing travelers to enjoy an unplanned drink at an airport bar or browse through the airport candy store.

Why it works

As the *Calibration Hack* (p. 82) showed us, we tend to underestimate how much effort we need to invest to successfully complete a task. Hackless humans make similarly optimistic guesses in all areas of life—everything from how long it will take to revise a resume to how quickly airport parking and security lines will move. At face value, these bad estimates seem to be based on an inflated view of our own efficiency. In fact, they are rooted in an overestimation of our *control* over our environments—we downplay the inevitable fact that life never goes as planned. As a quick glance at airline performance statistics shows, each day about 20 percent of flights are delayed. But almost nobody plans for this—we never imagine *our* flight will be affected. We seem hardwired to assume that we can circumvent the odds. The *Reality Hack* is different than the other *Action Hacks*, which focus on precise planning and anticipation of task obstacles. Instead, the *Reality Hack* asks us to see how improbable perfection is, and to think about how we can respond positively to negative events.

Instead of being sidetracked by the negative feelings that temporary inconvenience can cause, use the *Reality Hack*, which asks us to think about our perfectionism. Some of us believe that things must go exactly as planned for us to be satisfied. But this is both improbable (because rarely does anything go exactly as planned) and irrational (because many different paths can lead to the same goal). When things go wrong, we have a choice between a negative response and a goal-directed response. In the negative response, we attribute the delays, mistakes, and inevitable inconveniences we encounter to our own personal deficiencies—we think we must have handled this situation badly for it to go wrong. In the goal-directed response, we frame obstacles as opportunities to be productive and make progress toward predetermined goals. The *Reality Hack* is twofold: first, we acknowledge that things will occasionally go wrong no matter how hard we try, and second, we look at setbacks, mistakes, and disappointments as opportunities to try out different approaches in order to reach our goals. Ultimately, the situation does not determine our behaviors, emotions, or outcomes—we choose how we react to events that are beyond our direct control.

Application

The *Reality Hack* is most useful when a plan or expectation goes wrong. First, check to see if the situation is within your personal control. You can use the *Reality Hack* to control your responses

YouTube video:
Reality

when your political candidate loses or when the family picnic is rained out—events you can't personally control. But this Hack is more useful when the situation is, at least in part, within your control: being passed over for a raise or promotion, a breakup, not being recognized for an accomplishment. In these circumstances, you can avoid ruminating on negatives by focusing on the tactics you'll use to get better outcomes next time.

Instead of dwelling on the reasons for failure, channel the negative energy into a defined action plan for improvement: analyze your disappointment or failure and devise strategies to achieve the outcome you prefer next time. To use the *Reality Hack*, you must be able to describe in concrete terms exactly what that alternative outcome looks like, and then create the conditions needed to realize that goal. While the airplane delay example seems out of your control, there are plenty of benefits to unexpected time as long as you're prepared. To be prepared, you must first realistically assess the probability of something going wrong and make contingency plans. Then you'll be ready for reality to disrupt your plan.

30. Bridge Hack—*Attaining goals means closing the gap between a current and a desired state. Conduct a gap analysis before task engagement.*

The details

The job market twenty years ago was very different than what it is today. In the mid-1990s, when e-commerce companies like Amazon and Yahoo were emerging, jobs were plentiful, salaries were rapidly rising, and competition to hire the most qualified college graduates was ferocious. Sign-on bonuses were the norm, especially for candidates with technology skills, who frequently earned $5,000 to $10,000 (or more) for accepting a job offer. As a recruiting director for KPMG, one of the largest consulting firms in the world, I hired college grads with accounting degrees as financial auditors. One day my boss called me into his office to lecture me about my numbers. He shouted that the success of the entire division rested on my shoulders. If I couldn't hire three hundred people in the next three months, he threatened to decimate our division and my staff. My boss thought we could meet financial projections only by hiring more bodies. From my perspective, the problem wasn't hiring new people—it was keeping the ones we had. My boss failed to acknowledge the audit staff's 40 percent turnover rate; we were losing people faster than I could hire new ones. While I wasn't a mathematician, I *did* know that pouring water into a leaky bucket would not fill the bucket. We didn't need more hires; we needed to control attrition.

The *Bridge Hack* would have been the ideal strategy to resolve the KPMG dilemma. In this Hack, you conduct an analysis to identify the differences between what you have and what you want, and then you figure out how to reduce those differences—a process called *gap analysis*. First, evaluate which skills are essential for task success, and assess those skills against a measurable goal state. Then narrow the skill gap through personal development or training initiatives that enhance existing skills or teach new ones. In the KPMG situation, showing managers how to reduce turnover might have been a more effective and less costly strategy than recruiting new employees in a highly competitive job market. While gap analysis is usually aimed at systems-level interventions, you can conduct similar assessments to move you closer to your goals. We often assess our own skills subconsciously; the *Bridge Hack* formalizes the assessment process and outlines specific action plans to reduce the gap between who you are and who you want to be.

Why it works
Gap analysis is widely used to implement organizational change and improve individual and group performance. On a systemic level, gap analysis is used to identify organizational problems that can be mediated through individual actions. When employees collectively build skills, the organization grows stronger. The key to the process is using objective data to determine how each current competency differs from its ideal state, and to evaluate incremental progress using clear, objective, easily measured data points. Ideally, as new skills are acquired or existing skills refined, employees gain competencies and accomplish goals not possible before the intervention. The intervention's success depends on each employee's personal willingness to change, but it also needs strong organizational support, which is usually demonstrated by providing resources and time for personal and professional growth.

The individual gap-narrowing process is similar to the organizational approach, except you assess the skills you decide you need to develop. The gap analysis starts with deciding which of the three comparison points discussed in the *Anchor Hack* (p. 87) you will use: (1) besting your current skills or prior performance, (2) meeting a performance-specific standard, or (3) comparing yourself to another person. Skills assessments are subjective and vulnerable to thinking biases. Keep in mind measurement of progress should be highly objective. For example, if an individual conducting a gap analysis feels awkward around new people or in group social situations, they might decide that their sociability skills need improvement. They would measure their progress by assessing feelings of social confidence and competence. In this example, the formerly shy person might (mentally or physically) keep track of the number of conversations initiated, the number of times they remembered the names of new people, or how many ounces of alcohol they needed to feel comfortable approaching a stranger. The more objective the measure, the more likely you are to measure *actual* versus *perceived* change.

Application

The *Reality Hack* (p. 154) aimed to identify which aspects of life can be influenced or controlled, helping us respond positively to unexpected events. The *Bridge Hack* builds on the *Reality Hack* with a more tactical focus, helping measure how much your effort investments are paying off. There are variations on gap analysis, but most models define and prioritize what needs to change, identify an end state, and choose measurement and evaluation criteria to track progress. As with many *Action Hacks*, it may help to enlist other people's support for ongoing coaching and evaluation. Doing so will help your motivation and also help

YouTube video: Bridge

check personal bias, which can lead to inaccurate self-assessment. In other words, get a second opinion.

The *Bridge Hack* is especially useful when you need to develop or change fundamental work skill sets or develop personal and emotional skills, such as empathy, understanding, friendliness, assertiveness—any attribute that enhances competence or reduces personal anxiety. Be careful to avoid the nonproductive self-handicapping strategies described in the section explaining the *Mask Hack* (p. 146); work to find the root cause of any behavior you want to change. While it is wonderful to eliminate *symptoms* of personal inadequacy through behavior change, the *Bridge Hack* is most effective when you address *why* the undesirable behavior existed in the first place. In the social confidence example described earlier, knowing why the person felt awkward around people would predict long-term change far more accurately than simply measuring how frequently the person interacted positively with others.

31. Master Hack—*Create a master goal-directed plan that critically examines how you intend to reach your objectives.*

The details

Now that you've identified what you can change (using the *Reality Hack*) and analyzed the gap between your current and desired states (using the *Bridge Hack*), your next step is to devise a plan to reach your goals. It may seem obvious that you should plan before you act, but most people neglect the obvious—instead they drift haphazardly through life. This may sound pessimistic, but as we know from the *Inside Out Hack* (p. 114), some people don't believe they control their destinies. I often overhear students and colleagues saying things like "Everything happens for a reason," "He was in the right place at the right time," and "I'm just unlucky." As these commonplace beliefs show, many people see themselves as being at the mercy of circumstance.

Over the course of my forty-year career, I have interviewed over a thousand candidates for a wide range of jobs. Employers value dedication to a chosen career path, and to behaviorally test for career *planning* versus haphazard career progression, I regularly asked, "Tell me about how you decided to have a career in the field of XYZ," or "How did you find your job at company ABC?" Invariably, some people explained that they weren't sure about their college major, took a class, and became interested in a subject, which led them to a job and an eventual career; others found jobs by answering classified ads or through friends or family. The best candidates described carefully planned careers that progressed via deliberate choices to learn needed skills. Given the option, who would you prefer to hire: the "right place/right time" candidate, or the one who executed a step-by-step plan to accomplish their goals? The planner gets the job almost every time! Does my assertion that people should plan before acting still sound pessimistic?

Why it works

Goal-directed planning is an aspect of self-regulation—the process by which people actively set, monitor, adjust, control, and evaluate their levels of thought, emotion, and motivation in order to reach their goals. Planning is the first step in the regulation process; people use a series of evaluations to determine what they want to accomplish. After identifying potential goals, they assess how much challenge they are willing to accept, evaluate the skills they have or need to succeed, and decide where and how to allocate their effort. When well-regulated people doubt their capability or lack motivation to pursue their goals aggressively, they modify the goals. If success seems unlikely, they adjust goals downward during the planning process, bringing goals into alignment with their skills and abilities.

Skill assessment is another element of effective regulation. Skill assessment is an evaluation of the task itself and the skills required to carry it out, not of the person who'll be performing the task. Someone who feels highly confident in their success might unrealistically evaluate the gap between the skills they have and the skills they need. Ask yourself "What knowledge, skill, or ability is needed to excel at this task?" The answer will help calibrate you to the actual task requirements and diminish your focus on personal qualities; missing skills should be evaluated as referenced in the *Bridge Hack* (p. 157). The task-based gap assessment should go beyond knowledge and include essential strategies. For example, a runner planning for a long-distance race may *know* that she needs stamina to complete the race, but may plan or self-regulate poorly, expending too much energy in the first few miles and failing to finish.

Application

Are you about to start a project, master a new skill, or help someone else reach a personal or professional milestone? If so, the *Master Hack* can help. Begin the process by asking a series of questions. What are the primary objectives? What knowledge is needed to complete the task successfully? How will you solve problems caused by knowledge and skill deficits? Have you considered the strategies you'll need to complete the task? If you succeed, will you be able to pinpoint why, and will you be able to replicate the strategies you used? Using the *Master Hack* brings these answers to the forefront of consciousness; it asks you to reflect on and evaluate your plan before getting started.

Although the *Master Hack* focuses on specific tasks, the Hack can also be used for larger projects. For example, one of the best uses of self-regulatory strategies is improving your health and overall well-being. A master health plan sets goals about nutrition, exercise, personal commitment, and support from others. When you set specific, measurable targets, you can monitor your incremental progress and see when and where you need to make adjustments. Specific plans help reduce anxiety and the roller coaster emotions that come with massive lifestyle changes. Arranging external support can make the difference between success and failure. Beware of interference from people who don't support or don't know about your health goals. Not eating cookies is easier when people don't offer you cookies.

32. Mountain Hack—*Effort fluctuates during a task; plan ahead to manage inevitable motivational lulls.*

The details

To create an effective master plan, use the *Mountain Hack*, which teaches you to expect obstacles and to prepare to meet them. For example, let's say you are writing a book with a hard publication deadline. You know that effective writing requires subject mastery, planning, organization, perseverance, and the ability to overcome emotional resistance (writer's block). You've thought through these obstacles and planned how to overcome them—you've set yourself up for success. Then a phone call comes in, telling you that your child has died in an accident. Will you still be able to meet the deadline? This isn't a ridiculous example I made up to test you; it happened to me. Life sometimes intrudes on work, and, no matter how committed you are, interruptions can derail your success if you don't plan to handle them. You never know what kind of curveballs life will throw your way; sometimes all you can control is how you react. Preparing in advance helps you handle the inevitable moments when emotions, distractions, or interference from others get in the way of your goals.

As explained in the *Rest Stop Hack* (p. 97), high levels of task motivation cannot be sustained indefinitely, and breaks are essential for performance excellence. Understanding how motivation connects with self-regulation allows people to anticipate when their attention and effort might wane; it also helps them deal with these inevitable lapses in motivation by using self-control mechanisms. People should also think through how they will feel during these performance lulls; emotions can range from indifference to hyperanxiety. The more important the goal, the more intense the feelings when task progress stalls. By anticipating these feelings, people can short-circuit their frustration before it takes hold, redirecting their focus *away* from the potential negative feelings and *toward* sustaining their forward momentum.

Why it works

The *Master Hack* (p. 160) focused on the first stage of self-regulation, *planning*. Typically, we start a task because it will move us toward a desired outcome. To reach a goal efficiently, we must think through the strategies and methods we will use to get us there. The *Mountain Hack* addresses the next step in the regulation process, the *monitoring* step, which requires us to actively monitor our motivation and take measurable steps to sustain our drive. During this step, we actively invest cognitive horsepower in evaluating our performance on the fly so that we can deal with any effort fluctuations. This self-monitoring process, sometimes called "meta-motivation," pays attention to emotions such as anxiety, boredom, or interest as well as to the specific task motivation. People who feel that they aren't making enough progress, or who think their skills aren't up to the task, find their attention lapsing and fear they will fail. Environmental distractions (other, more appealing activities that you can see or hear) can become especially powerful at these moments, and can derail performance. Send your roommate to the movies, turn the television off, and check social media later. Hone your focus!

Monitoring also means ongoing strategy assessment: know the best strategies for the task, understand how and when to use the strategies, and know which strategies you will actually use. Although seeking help from more knowledgeable others is a valuable strategy, perhaps you avoid asking for help because you don't want to admit you are struggling—perhaps you think asking for help is a sign of weakness. Optimal monitoring happens when you realize that your preferred strategies are situational and will not work in every circumstance. Select a strategy that addresses the specific obstacle you're facing—one that is situationally appropriate and one you can stand to use. Strategies are not one-size-fits-all; interim goals and motives change as you move through your tasks, and the most comfortable strategy isn't always the most effective one. Figure out which strategy will work best for you in each particular situation, then apply it judiciously and use it relentlessly.

Application

The *Mountain Hack* is named so because finishing a difficult task is like climbing a difficult peak. Successful climbers must anticipate obstacles in advance, preparing for lapses in energy, variations in terrain, and equipment malfunctions. This Hack can be applied in any situation that has a defined, step-by-step process for task completion. Only you can decide which tasks to apply it to because task challenge is subjective. The *Mountain Hack* is unnecessary for some tasks. There is little need to manage motivation unless the task is extremely easy, which can produce boredom, or extremely challenging, which can produce disengagement or discouragement. Attention-grabbing tasks like watching a favorite television show are not likely to benefit from the *Mountain Hack*, because high interest sustains engagement.

The Hack is useful primarily for tasks that are not inherently interesting or that you are not confident about successfully finishing. Ask yourself, "Can I do this?" and "Do I want to do this?" If the answer to either question is no, you may need incentives to complete the task. For instance, many people dread routine chores like housecleaning and laundry, but because cleanliness is a cultural necessity, they do it despite the drudgery. The incentive is the social acceptability that requires clean clothes and a clean house. When you are bored with a task or obligated to finish it, focus on the benefits of task completion; forget about the process drudgery. When you reach the desired outcome, positive emotions (pride, competence, and personal worthiness) will be generated, no matter how small the task. Stop performance lapses before they start by using self-rewards: when you are finished, take a needed vacation or engage in some retail therapy. Along the way, restructuring your environment—taking the dog for a walk or turning on background music—can often make the difference between finishing and giving up. Ultimately, this Hack requires you to accept that motivation will always falter. You need to know how to maintain your momentum when the going gets tough.

33. Milestone Hack—*Create realistic and attainable interim goals to achieve long-term goals.*

The details

I have a sinister streak, but I only use it for good. I heighten my students' arousal, hone their focus, and make them feel just a little pukey by using the "foot in the door" technique on them. This strategy, usually intended to promote retail sales, can also be subtly applied to help people move past feeling overwhelmed. This tactic is designed to prompt agreement. First, you start a conversation by asking someone for an outlandish favor: "Hey Joe, can I borrow your girlfriend for three weeks? Mine is in the shop." This initial appeal is an intentionally ridiculous request that is designed to be turned down, but it increases the probability of getting a yes to a more moderate second request: "Hey Joe, can I borrow your hammer for a couple of days? Mine fell in the toilet." The absurd ask gets your foot in the door, and the more reasonable ask opens it the rest of the way. It works because most people feel bad for refusing your first request; since the second request requires less from them, they are more likely to say yes to alleviate guilt.

I use this technique to convince students that they can successfully complete complex semester-long projects that require great effort. Learners in new courses are often anxious when I give them their twenty-five-page course syllabus, which includes a detailed description of the required semester-long project. The

YouTube video: Milestone

project requires them to write about an unfamiliar topic, and they doubt their ability to complete the daunting task. I wait until they look pale and sick, and then I give them the more reasonable alternative: a scaffolded schedule that requires small chunks of the project to be finished each week, with guidance. These chunks are then combined into one document. After their collective sigh of relief, I explain why I tortured them this way: successful project management requires setting small, discrete, achievable interim goals and regulating your energy and motivation so that you reach them. I aim to teach my students more than content knowledge; I also teach them strategies for success, including how to convert seemingly overwhelming demands into small, manageable, attainable weekly steps that lead to long-term learning and success.

Why it works

There are two common types of goals: *ultimate* motives are satisfied when individuals reach a coveted end state, such as finding a life partner, getting a new job, or reaching a desired weight-loss target, and *instrumental* motives are incremental milestones achieved during progress toward an ultimate goal, such as going on a date with a desired partner, landing a job interview, or turning down a favorite dessert. The most common goal-setting mistake is ignoring instrumental motives and fixating on ultimate goals. We do this, in part, because we are trained to believe that it's easy to attain goals—we're told we just have to "put our minds to it" and we'll succeed. This attitude discounts a fundamental human weakness: our unwillingness to delay immediate gratification in favor of long-term benefit.

For many people, delaying gratification is actually painful (p. 189). A primary human motive is the attainment of pleasure and the avoidance of pain—whether the pain is physical (muscle exhaustion when exercising) or psychological (being nice to your boring in-laws), we don't want to endure it. But we must endure pain to achieve growth; in motivation, enduring pain means deferring our focus on the (pleasurable) ultimate outcome and focusing on interim milestones. All worthy pursuits require us to endure some form of discomfort, inconvenience, or frustration, and the *Milestone Hack* diffuses the pain of delaying gratification by shifting your focus to instrumental goals, which can be realized through moderate effort and then celebrated. Using this Hack gives two benefits: it reduces performance anxiety, and it sets up multiple short-term incremental successes. Successive small wins add up to a huge victory!

Application

Think about a goal you have been avoiding for a long time. Are you avoiding it because you think it's too challenging or it will take too much time or effort? If this is the case, you are in good company: according to some surveys, procrastination, the most common self-handicapping strategy, infects 90 percent of the population. The *Milestone Hack* is ideal for jump-starting these long-avoided projects. I remember meeting with a distraught student who was freaking out because she couldn't seem to pull together a series of ideas into a coherent course paper. When I asked her to tell me about the ideas that were giving her trouble, she gave me a blank stare. Eventually, she revealed that she had not yet thought about the points she wanted to make! She hadn't done any of the small steps of thinking through the individual ideas, but she was filled with anxiety over not being able to connect these nonexistent points together to finish the paper. It took a lot of persuading, but she finally gave in and agreed to try my crazy idea: she would write down each idea on paper before she tried to complete the entire project. (She did fine on the final paper in the end; the *Milestone Hack* worked!)

This Hack can be applied in any personal or professional situation where a goal seems unattainable, either because it's so big that it seems impossible or because we don't have the skills to do it. Perhaps you are dissatisfied with your job or planning a massive project. Temporarily forget about the long-term goal; doing so can unstick you and allow you to move forward. This Hack is also useful in your personal life, where it can help resolve relationship issues. Many couples stay in unsatisfying relationships because they just can't take that first step toward repairing or leaving the relationship. While it may seem impossible to resolve years of fighting or distance, taking that first small step—having a conversation about your dissatisfaction—can get you moving toward reconciliation or farewell.

34. Double-Dipper Hack—*Design tasks so that they serve dual objectives.*

The details
Life is full of competing goals. We can't play tennis and study for an exam at the same time. If we chill with friends or family on vacation, we probably won't have time to volunteer at the local homeless shelter. And often work obligations may trump exercising at the gym. We know from the *Investment Hack* (p. 105) that when we are deciding which tasks to take on, we evaluate each task's value

and its costs. We end up making serious, deliberate tradeoffs when we choose one person, place, or activity over another. Thinking about productivity this way—as a zero-sum game—allows us to put all our available cognitive and motivational resources toward completing one task at a time, without risking distraction or sub-par performance by dividing our energies. However, this may not always be the most efficient way to achieve results; sometimes we can achieve two goals at the same time.

The *Double-Dipper (DD) Hack* is designed to help you achieve multiple goals with the same investment of effort as that required by a single goal. The *DD Hack* reminds you to select tasks or create action plans that move you toward multiple goals with one action: learning a language while visiting a foreign country, reading while you are on an exercise machine at the gym, or choosing an academic project topic that feeds into your long-term career goals. The *DD Hack* can be used to great effect when structuring an internship; you can earn university credit for gaining valuable work experience. Caution: the Hack does *not* mean

YouTube video:
Double Dipper

trying to do two things at once, sometimes called "multitasking" by pseudo-academics. This Hack focuses not on momentary shifts of attention or effort, but on working toward two outcomes with one action plan.

Why it works

Most Hacks aim to help you achieve higher-quality outcomes or faster task completion than would be possible without the Hack. Some Hacks work on any task, but the *DD Hack* has limitations because of our brain architecture and how we think. Performance tasks can be clustered into two buckets. Some tasks, such as completing math problems or following directions, require us to reason and evaluate; these tasks require high effort. Other tasks, such as brushing your teeth or driving in good weather, can be successfully completed with minimal effort. Think about it: when was the last time you read the directions on a tube of toothpaste or practiced making left-hand turns? You probably can't remember because both tasks are routine, well-practiced, and habitual; these types of tasks let you spend your commute or morning routine thinking about what to wear, where to go for dinner with your significant other, or how to ask your boss for a raise. In other words, *under certain conditions*, you can accomplish multiple objectives without compromising quality. However, in situations that involve complex reasoning, multitasking is physiologically impossible.

Many people will ardently defend their multitasking skills—what they see as their ability to rapidly shift their attention back and forth between two tasks. But humans have a limited capacity to process information. We typically rely on both visual and auditory channels to process information, and these channels can be quickly over-loaded by cognitive demands—think about what happens when two people ask you a question simultaneously, or when you are try-ing to check your lottery ticket against the winning numbers while someone in the background yells out random numbers. We might *believe* that we can do two things at once with no negative con-sequences, but in reality, our performance is impaired and inferior when we try. However, we can successfully do two tasks when one or both are well-practiced, or *automatized*. Armed with this knowledge about how our mind works, we can appropriately apply the *DD Hack* to complete highly similar tasks that allow one effort to work toward two goals.

Application

Examples of the *DD Hack* in action include creating a shopping list while watching TV or listening to music, taking a cooking class while on vacation, or reading while eating your dinner. These types of examples leverage how we process information and avoid cog-nitive overload that can disrupt information processing. Personally, my favorite use of the Hack is when I do errands. Weather per-mitting, I figure out where I need to go, carefully plan my route, and pedal off on my bicycle, burning calories and increasing health instead of wasting gas and adding to my carbon footprint. It doesn't always work out—there are rainy days, and sometimes my errands mean bulky packages—but on most days, the Hack lets me complete necessary tasks and get in my day's workout.

The *DD Hack* can also be used for psychological and emotional development in a very concrete way. Many of us find social situations rewarding; work and social contact are not mutually exclusive. Think back to my daughter Rebecca, described in the *Social Identity Hack* (p. 122). Many of Rebecca's leisure and academic decisions take into account her strong social motivation. You can support a political cause and make important contacts in your community, you can attend an annual association conference and find out about a great job, and you can make friends while taking roller-skating lessons. Now that I think about it, I was using the *DD Hack* when I met my ex-wife Toni; I was working as an ID checker in a bar, intending to simultaneously make money and meet women. Maybe you too have been double-dipping for a long time without realizing you have been subliminally hacking your motivation!

35. Rear-View Hack—*Avoid procrastination by planning backward from a desired end state.*

The details

My last blood test came back with abnormalities. I was worried, so I went to see Dr. Asmar, a renal specialist, who suggested a kidney ultrasound. I reluctantly complied. A few weeks later, I returned to his office to receive my test results. Asmar knew I was nervous about the visit. As a doctor, he was obligated to explain the details of the radiology report. But before he explained the results, he assured me I was fine, alleviating my unjustified fears. Only then did he interpret the test results for me—technically, his primary job as a physician. I was delighted to see someone using the *DD Hack* in the wild. Asmar's keen perception of emotion and his holistic patient-centered approach demanded that he do more than just regurgitate medical information; he also made sure that my worries were abated. Like Asmar, I, too, was practicing the *DD Hack*:

listening to my results while looking out for new Hack opportunities. (In fact, Asmar's approach spawned the idea for the *Rear-View Hack*.)

My consultation with Asmar helped me realize that solving problems doesn't always mean starting from the beginning. If he had ignored my worry and followed routine protocols, focusing only on communicating the information in the medical report, I probably wouldn't have paid much attention to the details—I would have been too distracted by my anxiety. Asmar explained that when the prognosis is positive, he always tells patients his medical conclusion first, *before* discussing any test evidence. I immediately realized that his approach could also be applied to setting targets, planning projects, and avoiding missed deadlines. The Hack says that when we think first about a project's finished end state and then work backward to its current state, we are more realistic and aware of instrumental project milestones than we are if we start from the beginning and work forward.

Why it works

The *Rear-View Hack* can reduce procrastination. Why do we procrastinate? Students give all kinds of weird reasons: some say they work better under pressure; others claim procrastinating gives them more time for other activities, such as working and being with friends; still others say they aren't motivated to start a project that isn't due for many weeks or months. Some even believe procrastinating leads to superior performance (a misconception, biased by personal opinion and unsubstantiated by any real evidence, by the way).

People procrastinate for three reasons. First, as you may recall from the *Mask Hack* (p. 146), people create artificial protective barriers that they can blame if they fail, and procrastination is one of these strategies. We use it to rationalize prospective failure and justify actual failure. If our performance is weak or we miss a deadline, we can tell ourselves that we could have done just *fine*—if only we had started earlier. Second, we also struggle to accurately identify the actual problems we face; we jump to conclusions and solutions before we thoroughly examine the circumstances and nail down the *actual* problem. Third, we tend to rely on familiar strategies because novel solutions take effort and creativity. This explains why many people only apply for jobs by answering want ads, despite this tactic's miserable 4 percent success rate. These three challenges intertwine: it's more difficult to try new strategies with an ill-defined problem, and ill-defined problems and strategy stagnation cause procrastination. This is why it's so difficult to untangle why a qualified college graduate can't get a job interview, or how a young adult can maintain dignity and self-respect while living in their parents' basement. The *Rear-View Hack* mitigates all these challenges by asking you to envision the desired end state and trace a path backward to your current position. To carry out the *Rear-View Hack*, identify instrumental milestones, examine all conditions, materials, and supports that should be in place at those milestones, and then predict possible failure points: ask yourself, "What circumstances would prevent me from reaching this point successfully?" When you work backward, you focus on leaving nothing out.

Application

Using the Hack properly requires you to objectively analyze how long activities will take and how much effort will be needed, and to ask yourself "what if" questions to discover factors that might keep you from making your project milestones. In practice, the *Rear-View Hack* might be used to plan a wedding, navigate a cross-country road trip, or complete an academic project. This method also goes by other names, including backward design, reverse planning, the Mikado method, or the Critical Path process. All of these approaches ask you to visualize a project plan with multiple defined steps; you can't move forward until all conditions at the previous step have been met. Moving forward means figuring out *in advance* what might keep you from reaching the next milestone. Converting this philosophy into action means finding out how long the movie runs, making the right amount of popcorn to last you through the whole thing, and peeing before you sit down to watch. Be ready to watch the movie through to the end *before* you hit that play button.

If your project is more complicated than movie-watching, the Hack works the same way—you're just dealing with more details. Imagine you are the basement-dwelling college grad described earlier, and that you want out. First, envision your perfect job. Start by writing down the skills you need to do the job competently, the geographic location, the salary level, and where the position sits on the org chart. Next, systematically examine each area, comparing where you are to where you need to be. You may discover you need to gather more information, develop new skills, or (eventually) move. List the information you need, identify the skills and make a plan to develop them, research moving expenses and housing costs in the new area—nail down everything about these instrumental milestones as you plan, before you work back another step in your planning. If your systematic backward evaluation leaves you depressed, re-read the *Humility Hack* (p. 111); instead of dwelling on the obstacles holding you back, let those uncomfortable feelings motivate you to move forward.

36. Stone Tablet Hack—*Success is more likely when ideas are transformed into coherent written plans.*

The details

Romanian author and philosopher Emil Mihai Cioran once said, "Beware of the thinkers whose minds function only when fueled by a quotation." Plenty of people spout off motivational quotations, but few of them ever take the necessary steps to convert their ideas into actions. Dr. Feenstra once told me he wanted to invent disposable underwear for people who travel a lot. Another friend suggested child-free flights to separate cranky curmudgeons from crying babies and annoying children who kick the backs of airplane seats. I think that foldable, expandable smartphone screens would be highly practical and reduce the need for hideous computer monitors that eat our desk space. Do we have any of these things yet?

No. One reason great ideas don't get implemented is that we don't get the mental image out of our heads and onto paper; we need to turn ideas into concrete plans with specific, measurable milestones. Too many ideas never get past the stage of casual conversation over a glass of wine and shrimp-flavored potato chips (which, for the record, do exist, and are a little disgusting). Perhaps we don't act because we don't think the idea would pay off, or we think it would require too much effort (see the *Investment Hack*, p. 105). But when an idea has both high value and low implementation costs, some people act and some people don't. What is the difference between the dreamers and the doers?

Part of the success formula is simply writing things down. I have a file labeled "Brilliant Ideas" that holds a bunch of scraps of paper scribbled all over with ideas that have not yet become reality. (The last time I looked in the file, I could barely decipher my cryptic notes.) Writing things down isn't magic, though—filling folders with scraps of paper uses a very different skill set than creating and executing a plan to implement those ideas. Successful doers conceptualize an action plan to support thinking. Many of us are list people—we feel real satisfaction when we cross things off our lists because it gives us positive feedback (p. 177) and makes our progress more concrete. Some of us even write down routine daily tasks, like showering and dressing, because it helps us manage our time. These simple strategies may seem obsessive, but daily list makers tell me that marking off an item motivates them to accomplish the next item. Don't scorn those list makers; people who make lists have higher GPAs, accomplish more, and have better time management skills than people who don't make lists. So what should be on your list?

Why it works

Writing things down and making lists are regulatory strategies that increase learning and predict higher achievement. They work because they force you to actively monitor your own behavior. People who have a plan are more likely to stay on task than people who ricochet through their day like a pinball off the bumpers.

Monitoring works best with visual representations: logs and using journals are especially effective, because they track progress and record strategy use. If you keep a log, you'll be able to tell what strategies work best at each specific point in the performance cycle. The *Stone Tablet Hack*, which psychologists call the *trace* method, asks you to record not only your plans, but also the realities: what you did, what strategies you used, and what outcomes you got.

The *Stone Tablet Hack* enhances your recall. If you have trouble remembering to do certain tasks or following through on your ideas, the process of writing them down more deeply encodes that information in neural pathways. Thinking about something only imprints the information in the memory's auditory processing channel, but writing it down requires both auditory and visual encoding, forcing us to process information more deeply and making it more likely that we will successfully remember it. If you are like me, the act of writing something down is the key to memory, not the written reminder itself! You may not even need your notes once you've written them down.

Application

You don't have to be Santa Claus or Moses to use lists. Mere mortals can choose from literally dozens of ways to apply the *Stone Tablet Hack*. Daily uses include simple tasks like jotting a shopping list on the back of an old envelope, using a storyboard to track project plans, using your smartphone calendar or notes tool, or writing notes on a whiteboard with a dry-erase marker. The Hack can be used at any phase of a project. Before starting, list the knowledge or information you need to complete a task, the specific task goals, a timetable, and the blend of strategies you plan to use. During the task, keep a record of events, list needed changes and improvements, strategies for maintaining momentum, and what kind of feedback would enhance performance. After task completion, list the factors that should be evaluated, which strategies could be changed to enhance efficiency, and an objective assessment of how well you performed.

The *Stone Tablet Hack* can also help you monitor and track broader goals, including the daily challenges of maintaining a healthy lifestyle, enhancing personal development, or overcoming grief. Break the goal down into manageable parts (as described in the *Milestone Hack*, p. 165) and track your performance incrementally to enhance your motivation; when possible, publicly display your results to solicit feedback and recognition from valued others. People who track their weight, minutes of exercise, and blood pressure are more likely to recover quickly from illness, persist with exercise regimes, and score higher on ratings of personal well-being when their results are shared with others. The *Stone Tablet Hack* will enhance your performance and accelerate goal achievement.

37. Feedback Hack—*Engage in tasks that provide objective feedback. The more feedback generated, the higher the probability of task success.*

The details

Most graduate school admissions departments require an entrance examination to ensure potential students are "qualified" to pursue graduate study. I took the GRE under strange circumstances (p. 95). You already know how the exam turned out, and what a critical role feedback played in my test performance. As soon as the computer started giving me more difficult questions, my motivation hit a brick wall face-first. I was in a high-stakes situation, and my mind and body sent me urgent messages: my stomach churned, I was panting and sweating, and the mean little voice in my head was yelling, "Fool! You'll never get into grad school now!" and "You'll be the laughingstock of your family." At least the objectively generated feedback made me highly aware of how badly I was doing.

The Great GRE Debacle of 2002 is a terrific example of how external feedback influences performance. Computer-adaptive testing—the kind used on the GRE—adjusts question difficulty based on past performance. In other words, if you answer a series of questions correctly, the testing algorithm delivers harder and harder questions until you start answering wrong; then the questions become easier again. This adaptive method is exactly what happens in real life. If we attempt a series of tasks and fail, we are assigned (or choose) easier tasks. Performance feedback—either externally or internally generated—can be used to adjust performance or modify goals; seek performance feedback by using the *Feedback Hack*.

Why it works

Feedback comes in many shapes and sizes, and in *every* case, feedback links action to intention. Feedback externalizes our thoughts and feelings, and allows us to make comparisons between how we intended to perform and how we actually perform. You can respond to feedback in two ways: it either increases your attraction toward the goal and boosts your effort, or it decreases your motivation, leading you to either revise the goal or abandon it. Here's an example of how feedback loops work. One time when I was driving my family to a vacation on the Rhode Island coast, I was stopped by a police officer, who, in the words of my daughter, "gave Daddy some mail." My "mail" was feedback from the police officer in the form of a speeding ticket; his feedback caused me to drive much slower for the rest of the afternoon. Later that evening, I was sitting at a beach bar sipping on an icy Sloe Gin Fizz, and a beautiful young woman passed by and smiled. I immediately thought she dug me. I stared back, but she kept glancing away. I kept staring—giving her external feedback about how attractive she was. After about a minute of this, she picked up her belongings and scurried away. Twice in the same day I learned about how feedback can stimulate avoidance behavior.

Internally generated feedback occurs when someone consciously monitors their progress on a task, subjectively assessing their performance. I did this when I was taking the GRE: I thought about the test's difficulty, decided how I should allocate my time to finish the test in the time I had, and constantly evaluated the strategies I was using to answer the questions. My internal feedback about the questions' difficulty determined my engagement and effort investment: this is what drove the change in my goal, which went from "excel" to "pass." Internal feedback can also change task beliefs—especially beliefs about whether the task can be successfully completed. My internal feedback produced more and more guessing behavior. As the test went on, my motivation was severely tarnished; I also began to doubt the reliability of the GRE, because I was *positive* that I was grad school material, and the test wasn't reflecting that. In fact, external feedback is more reliable than internal feedback because it objectively compares results against standards and is less susceptible to bias. The best feedback is elaborative feedback, which explains *why* a response is right or wrong—much more useful than simply getting a big red X beside a wrong answer.

Application

Feedback is everywhere. When you drive, you use the speedometer to determine whether you can legally drive faster; if you see flashing lights ahead, you slow down. You arrive at the corner and completely stop at the red light. Maybe you look at your watch and get more feedback—are you early or late? You get feedback in the form of nonverbal cues from a partner or parent, who grimaces when you declare, "Justin Bieber is the greatest performer of all time." Even your pet provides objective, unsolicited performance feedback when they pee on the floor. Fido wants

YouTube video:
Feedback

you to know that you were gone too long. These feedback examples differ from performance feedback only in that they are automatic and require little effort to evaluate and act on.

To perform at our best, we must deliberately seek out feedback. The basketball player with two shots at the foul line uses feedback from the first shot (a swish or a brick?) to adjust her shooting motion for the second shot. The manager rethinks his interview questions when his seemingly perfect new hire quits after a week. The politician deletes his controversial Tweet after he's mercilessly trolled. These easy-to-recognize examples are low-hanging fruit, but other feedback opportunities are less obvious. Figuring out the answers to ill-defined problems (why were you not invited to the party? Your life looks so great on Instagram—why don't you feel happy? Why are you bored by activities that other people love?) involves systematic analysis and requires you to ask yourself the right questions. This Hack doesn't provide instant gratification, but it helps you move toward solutions using objective feedback, self-questioning, and analysis.

38. Vision Hack—*Close your eyes and visualize desired results to hone focus and predict outcomes.*

The details

Golfers lining up a crucial shot, pilots landing in bad weather, sculptors chipping marble from a block to reveal their ultimate creation, fashion models avoiding the humiliation of tripping on a runway, chefs mentally creating this evening's pièce de résistance—these people are all using the *Vision Hack*, and so should you. Visualizing a desired outcome promotes cognitive and motivational arousal that enhances performance. The brain gets a signal that reduces the lag time between the intention to act and the action. In the same way that preheating an oven primes it for proper baking, visualization prepares the brain to carry out a task.

Visual activation isn't just for athletes; it is just as useful in preparing for a presentation. When the stakes are high and reputations are on the line, even the best presenters can get anxious and freeze up. But don't think about what might go wrong. Envision yourself performing flawlessly. As you wait your turn, begin to mentally relax by imagining the event unfold. First, pretend every person in the room is intently fixated on what you say; their body language tells

OtmarW/Shutterstock

you that the audience is engrossed in your presentation. When you ask the audience a question, half of them raise their hands, hoping to respond. You are at the top of your game and everyone knows it. Run through the entire reel in your mind, right through to the end of the flawless presentation. Now it's time to relax and reflect on what you accomplished. Use the *Vision Hack* again to imagine how you will feel after your masterful performance.

Why it works

Imagery works because it generates perceptual information. Reading about a skill, or having it explained to you, only captures one dimension. To add depth to this kind of instruction, supplement the text with visual imagery (pictures, charts, or graphs); the brain processes abstract information less effectively than ideas grounded in concrete visual representations. For example, I could describe the *Double-Dipper Hack* (p. 168) to you at length, or I could simply say "you can kill two birds with one stone"—the visual image this evokes, of two birds' broken bodies, is more concrete and memorable than hundreds of words of explanation.

Although most of these examples discuss visual imagery, task performance can also be mentally rehearsed using other sensory inputs—auditory and kinesthetic projections. Different types of imagery work better for different tasks. You need at least basic knowledge of a process or skill to use kinesthetic visioning—this is what basketball players do when they mime shooting baskets before taking a critical foul shot. Combining multiple types of imagery enhances performance based on the premise described in the *Feedback Hack* (p. 177): using multiple input channels (visual, language, auditory, kinesthetic) deepens processing. In other words, the more ways we think about something, the more durable the mental representation we create. Imagery is also a form of practice, allowing us to reflect on what needs improvement.

YouTube video:
Vision

Application

Only you can decide when to use the *Vision Hack*. Ideally, the task should be moderately challenging but attainable. Visualizing a completely untried task is less effective, because you can't use experience to refine your skills, and visualization alone isn't enough to master an extremely challenging task. The *Vision Hack* is most effective when moderate anxiety is present—exactly the amount of anxiety you feel before a high-stakes performance for which you are well-prepared. Visualizing successful outcomes can help any time you feel uneasy or stressed.

A nervous student who is well-prepared for a final exam could envision writing flawless prose on an essay exam or being returned a graded test with an emphatic red A+ on the cover. Similarly, since performance motivation ebbs and flows, it's useful to visualize powering through motivational lapses. And workers might do well to envision recognition from peers and managers for a job well done. Visualizing can also be used to *decrease* nervous arousal: deep breaths and visions of serenity can work wonders!

39. Self-Talk Hack—*Literally talk to yourself to maintain focus and task engagement.*

The details

Remember fictional psychopath Travis Bickle talking to himself in the 1976 movie Taxi Driver? (Yes, I'm talkin' to you.) This is arguably the most chilling and memorable self-talk to be represented on film: in the famous monologue, Bickle is mentally practicing to commit a murder, talking himself up to ensure a masterful performance. You don't have to be planning a murder to use self-talk (in fact, I hope you're not). Positive self-talk is useful in any situation where self-doubt might inhibit success. Self-talk is strongly connected to superior learning and performance, and it is a great strategy for powering through temporary motivational lulls.

In the *Self-Talk Hack,* you psych yourself up, verbalizing your thoughts to convince yourself you have the skill and the intensity needed to succeed. Self-talk is especially useful for helping you maintain attention and focus. The strategy can be used in especially challenging or especially boring situations. Self-talk is most effective when you use your own name, when you focus the talk on a specific aspect of performance (on either motivation or skill, but not both at the same time), and when it is positive: "Now, Bobby, stop checking your text messages. I know you can complete this Hack now. Quit messing around!"

Why it works

Self-talk (also known as inner dialogue or an inner voice) can be direct verbalizations (speaking aloud to yourself), subvocal internal thoughts, or nonverbal representations of thought. Athletes who use self-talk perform better and are more likely to be selected for Olympic and professional teams than those who don't. The most effective forms of self-talk are positive verbalizations that focus on factors within a person's control and are targeted to specific aspects of a task: for example, telling yourself "You will get a hit if you focus your eye on the ball" works better than a general statement like, "You can do better."

Self-talk can also help regulate emotion that might negatively affect performance. Self-talk can work as a form of motivational self-control to temper reactions to an unfair world and keep the person focused on their priorities. For example, the football player about to kick a game-deciding field goal can say to himself, "Ignore the catcalls about your mother's promiscuity—you know all your siblings," and concentrate on the kick. These types of self-talk verbalizations should be aimed at regulating your effort and persistence when the going gets tough and we start to doubt ourselves. The *Self-Talk Hack* can focus on superior performance or on avoiding the embarrassment of failure. Self-talkers are more resourceful and use more varied strategies to accomplish goals than their silent peers. If you hear your coworkers muttering to themselves, they may not be insane; they may be encouraging themselves to perform their best, and you should model their behavior (p. 36).

Application

"OK, so how should I go about describing this example? Maybe I should tell a story about how to make a boring task more interesting, since being bored at work and school is a huge motivational problem." "Excellent point, Bobby!" (If you have ever been forced by a boss or a professor to do something you don't want to do, then you recognize this kind of self-talk.) "I know how I'll get through this article! I'll look for typos as I read. That will keep me focused and make this boring task more fun." "OK, let's go ahead and start counting. Just don't get caught up in it and lose concentration on the topic."

The *Self-Talk Hack* is useful for bolstering motivation; it's also useful when planning, monitoring effort, and evaluating strategy use. It's especially valuable in emotionally charged situations. Start by reminding yourself that you cannot perform at your best when your mind is hijacked by emotion (positive or negative). Imagine you are driving and someone cuts you off. The automatic response might be to explode in order to vent off the spontaneous anger. But honing your focus means blocking out intense feelings like anger, stress, and rage. Think or say to yourself, "Will this obstacle matter tomorrow?" "Is this worth getting upset over?" "Should I jeopardize my plans and possibly my future because of that idiot?" Ideally, you will grit your teeth and keep driving. Because the moment of self-talk introduces a pause, you have time to decide whether you are making the right choice; the pause also redirects your thoughts and emotions away from the bad driver and toward your goals. If you don't talk to yourself, start now! Only the uninformed will think you're weird.

40. Self-Consequating Hack—*Create unique and meaningful reward triggers to supercharge motivation.*

The details

In our world of extrinsic motivations, we are accustomed to doling out and receiving material rewards for appropriate behaviors. Schoolchildren who follow classroom rules are allowed to make a trip to the treasure box and pick out plastic choking hazards to honor their compliance. When kids behave at home, they ask their parents for privileges and treats (unless the parent indulges them with a reward first). Productive employees earn bonuses when they meet goals—and sometimes simply when they meet baseline expectations (like attendance awards, which recognize employees who show up for work). Consumers get into the mix too; insurance companies lower premiums for accident-free drivers, and loyalty programs reward regular customers with incentives like frequent-flier miles. In other words, for every action (or inaction) there is a reward, whether positive or negative. Some behavior elicits bling and some behavior (labeled by society as *mis*behavior) gets

Plastic juvenile incentives

penalized: a student gets an F for missing a deadline, a criminal gets a few months in jail for robbing a store. Rewards are everywhere in our society, but here's the irony: incentives determined by others rarely improve motivation.

The *Self-Consequating Hack* shifts the reward process to the individual, moving the locus of control. This Hack says that people should determine, when, if, and how their own particular accomplishments are recognized, ignored, or punished. *Self-consequating* means that each person creates their own consequences for actions; they work toward a particular milestone or performance threshold, and when they reach that threshold, they acknowledge their own achievement with a self-chosen reward. The concept is similar to the merit/demerit system (p. 9) I learned back at Nyack Boys School. If you meet your goals, you reward yourself: anything from buying magic tricks to taking a social media break—even booking a much-needed vacation after a long period of focused work, perhaps after finishing final exams or wrapping up a major work project. If you don't meet your goals, you can use negative consequation, or punishment. Rewards may be put off or eliminated: you may decline a party invitation in order to write for an extra thirty-minute block because the latest Hack is still unfinished. Experiment and find out which type works best for you.

Why it works

When rewards are external, they are controlled by someone besides the performer. As described in the *Option Hack*, lack of control reduces autonomy and motivation; when external rewards are removed, lackluster performance often follows. The *Self-Consequating Hack* changes the reward process, putting you in control of the reward system. You control *what* your rewards will be (no one knows better than you what you personally value and what you don't care about; companies' arbitrary incentives may be of little value to you). You control the decision about what task elements should be incentivized. This Hack doesn't work only for ultimate outcomes; it is equally useful for interim milestones like those discussed in the *Milestone Hack* (p. 165). Like many other *Action Hacks*, the *Self-Consequating Hack* is at its best when it's used to maintain momentum in the face of obstacles to progress or to discourage task abandonment.

This Hack is based on the same premises as most behavior modification programs: if a reward is satisfying, it motivates progress and increases the frequency of the desired behavior. To maximize the effectiveness of the *Self-Consequating Hack*, only reward yourself when you meet the predetermined performance thresholds. For example, if you decide that you will go away for the weekend after you get a job offer, you can't leave town merely because the interview went well. To be effective, the *Self-Consequating Hack* requires you to strictly adhere to your system of reward criteria, timing, and frequency, and to withhold rewards when goals aren't met. Self-control and personal integrity are *essential* for this Hack.

Application

I would give you some examples, but I am going for a bike ride because I finished the first two sections of the Hack. Actually, you must apply this Hack based on your own personal priorities. Don't let motivational gurus or karaoke academics tell you when, where, or how to reward yourself. Only *you* know what rewards are most meaningful for you. Following other people's instructions may mean the wrong tasks aspects are rewarded or the wrong rewards are offered. To use this Hack, decide first what is most important for you to accomplish, and how much frustration you can tolerate while progressing toward milestones. Use the *Self-Consequating Hack* and the *Stone Tablet Hack* (p. 174) together: think of two or three must-complete projects or tasks and write the tasks down, then determine logical performance milestones along the way for each task. Once you've determined the milestones, devise meaningful, attainable reinforcement triggers that will serve as targets, not as reasons to take breaks. Be sure you are willing to commit to the goal and select rewards that will work to stimulate your motivation.

At the same time, you should also consider a series of punishments. Now I don't mean you should plan to lick the nearest power outlet. Instead, you craft a list of things you *won't* do until you meet your designated milestones: being with friends or family, watching television, or reading additional segments of *Hack Your Motivation*. Keep sustainability in mind—how long can you reasonably keep working toward your milestone before you will need reinforcement? Realistic targets are far better than stretch goals, which lead to frustration that ruins motivation long before you meet your targets. Positive consequation—rewards—work far better to encourage persistence than punishment. Finally, don't keep your system, or this Hack, a secret. Share your plans with others to build in social support, which will help you follow your plan. You can power through obstacles even more efficiently when you don't want to disappoint your friends and family!

●

41. The DOG Hack—*Conscious Delay of Gratification enhances the likelihood of meeting long-term goals.*

The details

The prior *Self-Consequating Hack* doesn't work for everyone. Some of us are motivational superstars who don't need incentives to achieve earth-shattering results. If you have what it takes to forego distractions—if you can hone your concentration using the *Target Hack* (p. 131) and persevere through Herculean obstacles—then the *DOG Hack* is for you. In this case, DOG has nothing to do with Fido; it means *delay of gratification*. Using this Hack requires two qualities: self-control and the willingness to forego moderate satisfaction and benefits in favor of long-term glory. The DOG approach to task mastery assumes you have internal control beliefs (p. 114) and know that investing effort is the way to get results. To succeed with this Hack, you must also take responsibility for temporary setbacks and flexibly use multiple strategies to reach your long-term goals.

If you meet these criteria, then you likely already value long-term goals over immediate satisfaction. There is no precise way to measure your tolerance for delays in gratification, or how willing you are to give up immediate rewards for long-term benefits; as we say in psychology-speak, delay of gratification is subjectively anchored. Currently, psychologists measure someone's *delay disposition* (how likely they are to delay gratification) by offering choices and then observing what the person decides. Pretend you have earned a one-week all-expense-paid vacation to the Motivation Hall of Fame, located in Bisbee, Arizona, for getting this far into the book. You leave right now—put the book down and go! But let me tempt you: if instead you continue reading and finish the book, you will earn a *two*-week trip. What would you choose? To make the no-brainer decision—to finish the book and get a better reward—you must already have sustained confidence that you'll be able to master the rest of the material, strategies to get you through boring passages, and a complete understanding of the costs associated with *not* finishing the book (you'll miss out on important Hacks, people will whisper about how slack you are, and your friends and colleagues will shun you).

Why it works

The *DOG Hack* deliberately overrides Type 1 thinking (p. 72) by reducing reliance on intuition and suppressing impulsive behavior. Self-control develops at an early age, when children learn connections between their actions and predictable responses from others—when a baby with poopy pants cries, adults come running to change their diaper. As the child matures, they realize that they can regulate their own behavior to influence the behavior of others. In other words, the crafty juvenile learns conscious delay tactics help manipulate their world. The child who is patient and demonstrates good behavior gets a reward; the adolescent who studies diligently earns praise from parents and college scholarships; the working adult who perseveres when obstacles arise is promoted and recognized for their achievements. Research across disciplines and life phases indicates that when people can successfully delay gratification, they see enormous benefits. People who are patient and willing to defer temporary pleasure are less likely to abuse substances, are at lower risk for obesity, have higher standardized test scores, report greater overall job satisfaction, and show more substantial career growth. Waiting pays off (except when you skirt important deadlines)!

Considering this litany of positive consequences, how do we train ourselves and others to act DOG-like? The probability of embracing DOG increases when the specific, substantial benefits of delay are clear. Generalizations are not as powerful as knowing precise benefits: instead of saying "the more you study, the better grades you earn," explain that, while the relationship between years of formal education and lifetime earnings varies by gender, profession, and country, about 75 percent of earning potential is predicted by educational level. Another DOG training tactic is to offer visual evidence that makes the delay's benefits concrete: if you tell your kids you'll double their allowance if they reduce their computer time by half each week, make the abstract concrete by literally putting the extra money on the table where they can see it. People often choose immediate rewards over better long-term gains because the immediate reward is tempting and is in plain sight—right there in front of them. Put the cellphone away, close the Facebook window, hide the cookies in the cabinet—remove any environmental cues that might stimulate impulsive choices.

Application

Using the *DOG Hack* is primarily a value proposition, one that you must evaluate for each situation. The Hack can be especially useful as an overall control mechanism, reminding you that people who think and reflect on each choice and decision are more successful than people who react impulsively. Be judicious about when you use the Hack; some situations require quick decision-making, and in these situations, overanalyzing in service of delaying gratification might mean you lose an opportunity to someone else. Don't use the Hack to procrastinate and avoid making decisions. Use it only when deferral will actually result in a better overall outcome.

Although the *DOG Hack* is linked to well-being and other benefits, these benefits are not necessarily a direct result of the willingness to defer satisfaction; DOG hackers use different strategies to attain their goals than people who crave immediate satisfaction. Delayers usually have higher levels of intrinsic motivation, and they set and pursue goals to achieve mastery—not to look smart compared to others, but to develop and grow as people. In academic settings, learners who delay gratification elaborate more when they answer questions, are more organized, and think more critically about how to best learn and study; they are more aware of optimal learning conditions, and deliberately shut down social media accounts, turn off cellphones, and study in ideal locations. Ultimately, users of the *DOG Hack* think more about their futures and take specific, measurable actions that support their positive expectations.

42. Giftless Hack—*Great performance is best predicted by relentless practice, not innate ability.*

The details

Jameis Winston was a star quarterback at Florida State University. In 2015, when he was the #1 NFL draft pick, he landed a four-year, twenty-five-million-dollar contract with the Tampa Bay Buccaneers, including a sixteen-and-a-half-million-dollar signing bonus. Not bad for a twenty-two-year old with no professional experience. Many people see him as a "gifted" athlete. But is he really? In a 2016 interview, Jameis revealed that he, like most of his fellow athletes, started playing football daily at four years old and never stopped. Winston explained that his life, aspirations, and motivations were deeply entwined with football, and that all of his abilities and success were a function of his dedication to the sport. Jameis believes that excellence comes from focus and from intense practice, every single day. While we may believe athletic skill is an inherited quality—a "gift"—the *Giftless Hack* tells us that the difference between expertise and average performance is *practice*, spaced out over twenty-four-hour periods.

The *Giftless Hack* isn't exactly the same as the old saying "practice makes perfect," because it is not simple repetition that leads to expertise or professional-level skill. It is practice *plus* relevant, evaluative feedback, as described in the *Feedback Hack* (p. 177). Without expert direction and guidance, even a highly motivated person might practice the wrong thing, or practice the right skills in the wrong way. I see examples of strategy–practice mismatches in many contexts. At the gym, fitness enthusiasts use the correct equipment with horrible posture and poor form, inhibiting proper muscle development. In the classroom, teachers hoping to promote a collaborative learning environment spend most of their time lecturing, impeding the cooperation objective. Business leaders advocate empowerment while they explain the latest corporate policy mandating employee behavior. The *Giftless Hack* advocates consistent practice, but only when practice is benchmarked to industry, discipline, or professional standards.

Why it works

Although it's not included in the Motivational Myths and Misconceptions section (p. 49), there is a very common misconception about the origins of superior ability and expertise. Many of us believe good teachers, superior athletes, leaders—you name it— are born with certain qualities that predispose them to excellence. Although genetics help shape our intellectual and psychological makeup, it is irresponsible to assume that genetics alone are sufficient (p. 65) for excellence in a particular skill. Expertise comes from a combination of biology and the motivation to develop inborn talents. Without refined practice—practice with expert feedback— any inborn abilities remain dormant, like seeds planted in a pot in a dark room and rarely watered. Without ideal environmental conditions, even the best seeds will not grow, whether we are talking about plant seeds or the seeds of human potential.

Despite the overwhelming evidence for spaced practice (regular, frequent practice or learning sessions spaced out over time), some people still believe cramming works. These crammers' beliefs are unsupported by evidence, and are usually a function of the crammers' need to seem more talented and successful than their peers. (Cramming also offers a built-in excuse for failure.) Spaced learning and practice is supported by cognitive science and neurological findings. Repeated exposure to the same material, with at least a fifteen-minute lag between initial and subsequent learning, increases synaptic activation and more deeply ingrains neural pathways. When a person practices over time, recall is more reliable, with a higher probability of neurological distribution, than when learning is packed in all at once during a cramming session.

Application

The *Giftless Hack* is most useful in situations that require repetition to hone a skill. In learning situations, this might be when you are memorizing facts, learning a new language, or trying to master mathematical formulas. In social situations, you might use it when trying to match names and faces (as when you join a new organization or meet new people), commit directions to memory, or master a procedure (such as putting a watermark on an electronic document). All types of athletic performance benefit from the Hack's regular, spaced practice. Athletic skills require your body to memorize, or *automatize*, particular actions, developing the muscle memory that enables you to perform skills correctly every time without conscious thought. As an aspiring marksman, my training plateaued until I was able to automatize the procedures of shooting, including proper stance, grip, arm position, and safety protocol.

Reaching expert level with whatever talents you inherited requires three things. First, it requires a time commitment: ten thousand hours of dedicated practice, which are enough to give you a vast repertoire of knowledge and application in whatever field interests you. The key word here is interest; without interest and motivation, few people could sustain engagement over such a long period. A second prerequisite for expertise is the ability to apply your knowledge. Someone who has read hundreds of books on ice skating but has never stepped onto the ice will not be competent. Perhaps you know people who tell you, loudly and often, how competent they are at something, although they have no objective evidence (actual experience and results) to back it up; these people are usually anxious, insecure, and have low self-esteem, and they use their false expertise to boost their egos. The final requirement for expertise is an ongoing commitment to stay current in your field. You can't work in a field today based on expertise you developed thirty years ago. That's no different than thinking you can still buy a quart of milk for twenty-five cents: it's not happening.

●

43. Water to Wine (W2W) Hack—*When you keep your emotions in check, the worst things in life can still move you forward.*

The details

How can you lose twenty thousand dollars in five minutes and be happy about it? People usually think this is a trick question. No one likes to lose money. But with the right approach and the *W2W Hack*, any situation, however awful it seems, can become a positive motivational experience. This Hack teaches us how to manage the emotions sparked by the inevitable disasters of life: losing money, job termination, grief from the deaths of friends and family, and dozens of more mundane sorrows. We all know people who always seem to be having a bad day, and other people who are generally upbeat, optimistic, and enthusiastic, despite having the same problems as everyone else. The difference between the constant complainers and the habitually happy is driven by two motivational beliefs: the realization that things will not always go as planned (see the *Reality Hack* [p. 154] for more on this), and the understanding that we can control and regulate our subjective responses to life's tragedies, disappointments, and curveballs.

The answer to my riddle is simple. If you take a risk and fail, you want to minimize your losses, right? That is exactly what my friend Alec Torelli does when he plays professional poker. By the time he was twenty-seven, Alec had earned over three million dollars from poker tournament play. Alec sometimes loses large sums of money because he cannot control the cards he is dealt. But he does control his *response* to his hand. If he knows he cannot win and folds, he has made the right decision in a hopeless situation. He might have lost twenty thousand dollars on that hand, but he kept himself from losing two hundred thousand, so he's happy to see the smaller sum go. Like poker players, we can convert negativity into useful outcomes by focusing on improving ourselves rather than ruminating about life's unavoidable misfortunes. You may have noticed this book is dedicated to my late son Robert, who died

Alec Torelli

unexpectedly at age thirty. How could this tragic event possibly be positive? When Robert died, I fully realized all of his numerous wonderful attributes—things I had sometimes not noticed or taken for granted while he was alive. I modeled his best behaviors and began to teach others his kind ways, and so began to transform a parent's most devastating emotion, grief for their child, into a positive legacy. The *W2W Hack* takes practice, but a person who is aware and perceptive can repress spontaneous emotional reactions, stop rumination in its tracks, and aim their energy toward constructive resolutions to terrible situations.

Why it works
Believe it or not, bad things will happen to you. Failure, disappointment, and rejection are part of life. People react to misfortune

automatically—many physical and psychological responses are beyond our control. We may show typical avoidance behaviors and feel nauseous, confused, shocked, distraught, or angry. But after a few minutes, we begin to reflect on what has happened, and start to try to cope. Our coping behaviors come from patterns of behavior learned over the course of our lives. In other words, we make a choice about how to cope based on what we know. Some people dwell on the negative consequences; they might see losing a job as a deflating end point, not an opportunity to succeed and make more money elsewhere. These people will direct their cognitive horsepower toward quelling the negative emotions rather than toward achieving future goals and objectives. They might try to mask or disguise (p. 146) the emotion with nonproductive self-handicapping strategies like drinking or substance abuse. This type of coping may squash the feeling, but it offers no real recovery from the event.

Others consciously and deliberately regulate their emotions by redirecting the energy hijacked by the emotion into something productive, aiming to transform the negative situation into a positive outcome. This second coping strategy does not mean the uncomfortable emotion disappears, but it does shift the focus off the feeling and away from the event, which can't be changed no matter how awful you feel about it. This Hack asks you to realize that your emotion is nonproductive and doesn't help you recover; rumination wastes energy that we could use to focus on our goals.

YouTube video:
Water to Wine

Sometimes redirecting our energy is the only aspect of recovery we can control, and our only way forward is to work toward previously set goals or to be motivated by the event to create new ones.

Application

The grief recovery example I've used is a monumental and extremely difficult use of the *W2W Hack*. Start small. Think of what annoys you most. Maybe you get peeved when your spouse runs the washing machine when you are in the shower, dousing you with ice water. Maybe you're prone to road rage. Maybe TV commercials showing sick children or abused animals make you feel hopeless (they do me). But you don't have to fall in line with the advertiser's goal and contribute money to get rid of the negative emotion. Try the *W2W Hack* instead. Close your checkbook, redirect your cognitive horsepower, and volunteer your time, talk to others about how to help, or incorporate the cause into other meaningful goals, such as educational or career plans. Do anything that leads to goal progress, which will make you feel good.

However you apply the Hack, it's crucial to direct your focus *away* from the emotion and *toward* a productive outcome. To cope, you must affirm to yourself that you can influence your environment. If you doubt you can bring about the life outcomes you want, you will be more easily sucked under by the dark tides of emotion. Worry and stress come out of familiar, stereotypical patterns of coping that are easy and require little conscious thought. Avoid reactionary indulgence in the form of excessive eating, drinking, substance abuse, or other vices; instead, direct conscious, focused effort toward productive goals. Adaptation takes work. Despair will linger unless your intentional actions produce change and achieve your goals. Remember what you value, and use the Hacks to get what you want.

44. Bio-Social Hack—*Actively cultivate relationships. Socializing sparks the same neurological response as material rewards.*

The details

I need your opinion. I am planning a Hack Your MO party and deciding who to invite. Would you accept an invitation? The decision about whether or not to accept a party invitation can promote angst, even in the most confident, laid-back people. What factors might influence your decision about the party? We know from the *Investment Hack* (p. 105) that first you will decide whether there is a practical value to attending. You might consider things such as who will be there—perhaps you would make new business contacts, or maybe it would be useful to meet other motivational hackers. You would also consider the costs, and I don't mean the price of admission. Maybe you have something better to do that night, or you want to avoid feeling uncomfortable in a place where you don't know anyone else. Maybe you still believe the labeling myth (p. 55)—you don't realize that there are no types and that motives constantly change, so you see yourself as being too introverted to attend. Or maybe you are motivated to avoid other people, and you won't attend because it would be too stressful.

The *Bio-Social Hack* reveals that, although some people are reluctant to join social situations, our brains see social connections as highly fulfilling. Perhaps people who see the cost of attending as greater than the perceived benefits don't know the actual value of connecting with other people. Frequently turning down invitations is a form of self-handicapping. It is a deliberate avoidance strategy that conceptually serves the same purpose as procrastination ("I would fail anyway"), defensive pessimism ("the party will stink anyway"), or rationalization ("I wouldn't get anything out of going"). The reasons you give for not attending may be a mask (p. 146) disguising insecurity and anxiety—feelings you would overcome if you went and had a nice time.

Why it works
Socializing activates neurotransmitters and hormones in the brain; if the social situation is perceived as satisfying, the brain produces the pleasure hormones dopamine and oxytocin. Positive social interactions produce a biological reaction almost identical to the one we have when we earn money, learn new things, or fall in love. (The same feelings are produced by various drugs; this is why people who don't generate positive emotion in productive, socially acceptable ways may abuse substances.) These hormones cause feelings of contentment and general well-being. Those positive feelings get linked to interacting with other people, feeling confidence, serenity, and euphoria. Talking, laughing, and commiserating with

others is a rewarding experience that satisfies our strong affiliation motive.

But when a gathering is stressful, anxiety develops—not necessarily from the actual event, but from anticipating the event. Instead of releasing chemicals that produce feelings of warmth and contentment during interaction, the brain generates cortisol, a hormone connected to feelings of aggression, dominance, and competition. Biologically, social rejection stimulates pupil dilation, higher blood pressure, and a rapidly beating heart—fear responses. The person interprets these responses as meaning there is something to fear—their anxiety is very real. Controlling this negative reaction takes perseverance and practice, as well as support from others. The *Bio-Social Hack* trains your body to expect interactions to lead to positive outcomes and feelings. Even when there is initial reluctance, connection (even involuntary connection) is a foolproof remedy to overcome the fear of social inadequacy.

Application

When deciding where and when to use the *Bio-Social Hack*, remember that this Hack is based on the physiology of emotion: when you use the Hack, your heart rate and blood pressure should go down, producing feelings of contentment. As the body relaxes, positive emotions such as joy, elation, and happiness are triggered. The best time to use the Hack is when you feel down and lonely and desperately need a mood change. The mood change after socializing is so intense that connection is said to have an "undoing effect"—this Hack is powerful enough to alter our perceptions of ourselves and the world. When we feel better about ourselves, our moods rise and we become more open, honest, creative, and willing to accept divergent opinions.

Since we humans need to socialize, and since successful affiliation has such predictable positive consequences, the question is not whether to use the Hack, but when. What type of context produces the best bonding experiences? It's completely subjective, but relationships are more likely to be successful when all parties have shared interests. You can use the Hack successfully in any situation where you can seek common ground based on preference, values, or similarities, attraction will develop. Some obvious bonding locations include clubs, sporting events, cultural activities, and school because in these situations participants will have goals and perspectives that align with your own. We are most strongly attracted to nearby people who we see as similar to us in appearance and intelligence. Now, RSVP to my invitation, seek out someone who looks like you and is from your home state, and wait for the magic to happen.

45. Relocate Hack—*Reinvent how, when, and where you concentrate to avoid or eliminate unexpected attention lapses.*

The details
Imagine you are taking a graduate school entry exam like the GRE or the LSAT (the law school admissions exam). When you study, you always follow a methodical routine. First you arrange your books, notes, and study materials and pens, paperclips, sticky notes, and highlighters. Then you grab your favorite beverage and sit at your desk, primed to master the content—you want a top test score because you highly value admission to graduate school. This was explained by the *Investment Hack* (p. 105) and *Target Hack* (p. 131). You begin studying. Then your roommate opens your door without saying a word and closes it again. You are distracted. You attempt to concentrate, but your head pounds and you mysteriously lose focus. You try and power through the unexpected interference, but give up after ten minutes. Perhaps you take a nap—you justify stopping because you feel you know the material, and you rationalize that your brain probably needed a break.

Intrusions are a reality of life, but interruptions can change even intense drive and concrete plans into a heap of wishful intentions. We cannot control the external world, but we can regulate our reactions to distractions. This is partially explained by the *Self-Talk Hack*

(p. 183), which focused on controlling intruding emotions. There are other restructuring strategies in our hacker's toolbox that can help us maintain cognitive and motivational focus when conditions are tough. The *Relocate Hack* is designed to help maintain focus and targeted effort in chaotic situations. The strategy options include remedies such as changing where you work to eliminate commotion, knowing which time of day you perform best and doing your most demanding work then, and creating an optimal performance context (controlling temperature, light, and other physical sensations, including sitting in a comfortable chair at the right height for your desk). This Hack requires you to monitor the changing physical conditions that may impact your performance, and to pay attention to which conditions stimulate your optimal productivity. Just because one person works effectively in solitude doesn't mean you won't perform better listening to background music. Remember, contextual generalizations made by others are often wrong.

Why it works

When my daughter Rebecca was in second grade, I tried to show her a new way to solve multiplication problems. She responded by telling me, "Dad, all my slots are full!" She meant that she couldn't absorb anything new because she was on mental overload. While Rebecca knew nothing about cognitive science, she was on the right track. Humans have a limited capacity to process and store new information, and it is essential to eliminate any external distractions when learning or performing. If we are distracted by things like poorly designed instructional materials, bad teaching, cluttered desks, too-cold or too-hot offices, and interruptions from people, pets, and social media, we can't bring all our mental resources to bear on the task at hand. Some of our limited resources are put toward the distractions, and the task plus distractions requires more effort than the task alone would. We exert more effort, producing frustration and fatigue, often leading to motivational declines; routine tasks transform into hard work needing monumental effort.

To counteract interruptions, we need to know which of our idiosyncratic preferences actually contribute to optimal performance and when we can (and should) make a change. Before redesigning your work environment, consider how much control you have. Be realistic. It would be ridiculous to think you can reorganize the protocols that control an entire office building or lecture hall for your convenience. Expecting to go into a classroom and convince the teacher that homework is useless or suggesting that a company convert existing cubicles into offices for more privacy would raise eyebrows and get nowhere. However, you might get somewhere by suggesting a change in the *type or frequency* of homework assigned, or by coming to work early, before colleagues arrive. You probably can't change the temperature settings for your whole high-rise office building, but you can bring a sweater to work.

Application
The best time to use the *Relocate Hack* is when your expectations don't match up with reality. This situation often happens when plans go awry based on external interference. My most memorable moment of this kind of mismatch happened when my professor friend, Alex, asked if he could stay at my house over winter break. I agreed, but Alex hadn't told me about his charming, high-energy three-year old, who spent most of the weekend chanting "Uncle Bob, Uncle Bob" at me while dismantling my home and testing my patience. Productive writing during Annabelle's visit was as

Sweet Annabelle

unlikely as Donald Trump voluntarily attending a climate change summit. I could not concentrate even during the rare periods of quiet. I knew I needed to make some changes or my entire break would be unproductive. I found a secluded spot to write, lent Alex a car to go sightseeing in, and spent lots of time exercising to relieve stress. More importantly, I acknowledged the need for a change in order to meet my writing goals. Taking a break wasn't an option, and I couldn't modify my curmudgeonly personality.

Use this Hack when you have a looming project deadline—something like writing a paper or finding a job—instead of trying to renegotiate or postpone the deadline. Using the Hack takes resourcefulness, awareness, and an unwillingness to accept the status quo (p. 108). While you could just give up, that would likely generate negative emotion and damage your motivation for similar tasks in the future. Environmental restructuring goes beyond altering the physical working space. You can leave your annoying roommate behind by changing locations, but you would still have to deal with the psychological fallout of the interruptions. Restructuring your thinking process means creating conditions that allow you to ignore distractions despite the ongoing actual or perceived chaos.

●

Action Hacks are the key strategies that keep the motivational hacker energized and on target. Each Hack has situational relevance—besides knowing how to use each Hack, the user must also know when each Hack works best. Determine which Hack is applicable based on an objective assessment of key goals, of the performer's knowledge and experience, and of the relative value of the goals. Used appropriately, the *Action Hacks* help you reach your goals efficiently, fostering feelings of confidence and accomplishment as you make progress. Once the *Action Hacks* are mastered, the seasoned hacker can then focus on helping others achieve their goals with the Hacks.

CHAPTER SIX

Reflection Hacks

MOTIVES, LIKE MOST OTHER human traits, constantly change. Motivational change is not as predictable or as obvious as physical growth, but it impacts how we navigate the world. Our aspirations and self-expectations evolve as we encounter success or failure; we improve as we reflect on and evaluate *why* we succeed or fail. To grow, we must be flexible with the strategies we use, abandoning comfortable approaches that do not work and trying new strategies. This final group of Hacks examines how we reflect, how change leads to personal growth, and what we should consider before shifting our motivational gears.

46. Reframing Hack—*Motivational change has a starting point. Evaluate who sets the standards you hope to achieve.*

The details

Your response to challenges is shaped by how you see and think about them; you make decisions or choose strategies based on how you frame the issue in your mind. But before we investigate these mental frames in detail, let's have an argument—not an emotional battle based on political or religious ideologies, but an intellectual debate. The goal here is to give your opinion about health insurance. How long should children should be covered under a parent's policy? We will assume that the current United States law at press time (dependents can remain on their parents' policies until age twenty-six) is still in force in our argument. Because it is hard to find a job that pays well and has good benefits, and because children now live at home for longer periods of time than in previous generations, I personally believe that dependents should be able to remain on their parents' health plan until age thirty. Is my argument sound? Does it appeal to you? Will you support my change initiative? Your answers to these questions are probably "yes" if you are one of the many Americans under thirty who are uninsured.

Now pretend you are a citizen of Finland, where residents have lifelong universal health care paid by the government (through taxation). What if I told you that I believe the Finnish system should end the government subsidy at age thirty? After all, by the time someone is thirty, they should be gainfully employed and able to fend for themselves. Is this second proposal appealing? Both proposals are identical—both end health-care subsidies at age thirty. But the second idea is probably not as appealing as the first one. Congratulations, you have just been framed! In other words, your feelings about this issue were influenced by how the information was presented to you. Because free coverage is available for life in Finland, the proposal that seemed great to US readers would seem terrible to Finns. Framing can influence your motivations and your choice of strategies.

Why it works

Framing is nothing more than a crafty way of presenting information. The key to successful framing is to intentionally choose where the thinking process begins. There are frames—starting points or assumptions—that we accept without questioning them. For example, in the United States, two-week vacations are the norm, but in Europe (although standards vary by country) workers take four weeks per year; a European offered a contract that specified two weeks' vacation would probably reject the offer. At school, our frames tell us that the teacher is omnipotent and always right, that a visit to the principal's office is terrifying, and that it's really cool to date the quarterback of the football team or the head cheerleader. Step outside your frames, though, and you may find each of these premises is flawed: teachers can be wrong, some principals are supportive, and the quarterback may be much less

YouTube video:
Reframing

fun than the guy in the chess club. Frames have material impacts in the real world, too. In Las Vegas, a roulette bettor may choose black because the previous ten spins were red, or a card player may increase a bet because they feel they are due a certain hand. These gamblers are working within flawed frames; odds advantages are mathematical propositions that have nothing to do with previous events or magical thinking. Despite knowing how probability works, many gamblers use inappropriate frames to justify their betting behavior and wind up losing money.

We base our implicit beliefs about motivation on culturally learned frames that we rarely examine. For example, people are raised to believe that we should volunteer time to help others, that the underprivileged should be subsidized by the rich, and that everyone should have a quality education (whether they want one or not). Our opinions and motivated behavior are influenced by these frames; instead of deciding *if* you should volunteer, the frame may determine *how much* time you are willing to donate. The fallacy of framing dictates that unless we deliberately reflect on the premises we use to make decisions and analyze how we satisfy our drives, we may be suckered by other people's framing of important issues. Framing is not the same thing as social comparison; frames don't develop from emulating other people, but from long-term conditioned thinking based on popular media, on philosophical or religious dogma, and on cultural norms.

Application

According to the Work Group for Community Health and Development at the University of Kansas, framing dictates thinking, determines who is responsible for action, and controls what problem solutions are seen as possible. All *Reflection Hacks*, including the *Reframing Hack*, require you to objectively and critically evaluate a recent accomplishment or failure and make appropriate changes in response. Let's say you failed on a job interview or lost a heated political debate on Facebook. In each of these examples, you would reframe your next try: find common ground between you and your rival, present the right kind of evidence (evidence that your opponent values and finds convincing) to support your point, make contrasts and comparisons, and revise your persuasion effort to appeal to how the other person thinks about the subject. In your next job interview, don't boast about yourself; move the frame and inform the recruiter about competitors' strategies and the consequences of losing qualified candidates. Handle your next political discussion better: next time, clearly articulate the merits of your argument while at the same time boosting the ego of your intellectual foe.

If you frame your personal issues using shared public frames, you may shortchange your personal growth or strive toward goals that don't fit your idiosyncratic beliefs (a common experience for anyone who wanted a college major in art or dance but ended up pre-med). Use the *Reframing Hack* to evaluate whether your goals serve your own aspirations or external expectations. Is being childless at thirty selfish or strategic? Should you choose a career based on parental coercion or on personal satisfaction? Question the basic assumptions that drive your evaluations using the *Reframing Hack*. You might find that who you are, what you have accomplished, and what you are working toward are all perfectly fine, even if they aren't conventional or don't live up to other people's arbitrary expectations.

47. Against the Wind Hack—*Deeply question easy or popular strategies. Acknowledge that there are multiple methods to accomplish similar goals.*

The details

Students learn best in their preferred learning style. The ideal way to master a language is through constant repetition. Hyperactivity in children can be avoided through sugar-free diets. Do you believe any of these statements? These well-known "facts" are all false— they are *misconceptions*, or personally held statements, ideas, and beliefs that conflict with established scientific evidence. There are several reasons people might continue to believe false information. Myth 6 (p. 60) explained the evolutionary benefits of seeking simple, predictable explanations of events. The *bandwagon effect* suggests that people go with the flow of popular opinion (even if it's wrong) to satisfy affiliation needs. We prefer to surf the wave of popularity when the opportunity exists. Every teenager has probably said, "I want to go to (insert location), Mom, because (friend's name) is going." And every parent has probably responded, "If (friend) jumped off a bridge would you do that too?" People tend to adopt popular ideas—we exhibit herd behavior to avoid conflict and blend in. Some of you may still have shirts with double-pop collars or high-waisted Abercrombie jeans tucked away in your drawer; herd behavior is the *only* possible explanation for these nineties fads.

But none of these approaches explain why people cling to motivational strategies that don't succeed. People repeatedly try to use the same approach to resolve motivational challenges even when it's clearly not working. We've all heard that "insanity is doing the same thing over and over again and expecting a different result" (a quote erroneously attributed to Albert Einstein—another misconception). Some of us are insane, then. I know a frustrated job hunter who spends most of her time answering internet ads; she sends out emails and electronic resumes and... waits. This highly personable woman has been looking for a professional job for several years. Despite her many years of relevant work experience and a master's degree, she rarely even lands interviews. Yet she continues to answer ads by email—a strategy with a 3 to 7 percent success rate, depending on the source you consider. In reality, as many as 85 percent of new jobs are found through networking with people in your career field, but knowing this information has not motivated my job-seeking friend to change her strategies.

Why it works
Using the *Against the Wind Hack* means reflecting critically on easy-seeming or frequently used strategies to see how well they are really working. There are several reasons that people use the same strategies over and over even when they no longer work. The most common is the thinking bias called the *sunk cost fallacy*. When we feel that we have invested time, energy, or financial resources into a goal, we often internalize that goal and feel connected to it. But the days or weeks invested in a product, person, or idea do not

obligate us to keep working toward that goal. We can never recover our previous (sunk) investment of time or money—those costs are already gone. The only way to save a sunk-cost situation is to cut your losses and *stop investing more energy*. Plenty of mediocre financial and personal relationships linger on because of this kind of thinking.

Another reason for strategy complacency is *functional fixedness*, or what I call the go-to mistake. Functional fixedness means that we fail to consider new (potentially better) approaches to solving familiar problems. You can't fall asleep—what do you do? Reach for the medicine cabinet? Drink some warm milk and eat cookies? Lie in bed and read a book? You probably have a favorite solution that calms your restless energy. Next time, how about trying something new to cure the problem—two minutes of breathing exercises or a new routine of going to bed at a consistent time may work better. We fall into functional fixedness with motivational challenges as well. Unable to find a job? Many of us resolve the frustration by complaining to friends. Instead of the group hug approach, what if you collectively examine what you each do best and start a business together rather than complaining? People also stick to easy solutions because of ego, as explained in the *Mask Hack* (p. 146). Considering new approaches that may fail means removing the mask; it is far easier and emotionally safer to hide behind a comfortable, easy approach that produces no anxiety, even if it also produces less success. The job seeker who only answers ads does not have to experience the social anxiety of networking or the embarrassment of being rejected by people they know. The visual learners can tell themselves they are capable despite poor performance if they are taught through nonvisual modalities. Vulnerability comes with mask removal, but adversity stimulates growth, and it's difficult to grow behind a mask.

Application

The *Against the Wind Hack* is most effective at helping you reject familiar, yet unproductive, patterns of motivated behavior. The first step in using the Hack is acknowledging dissatisfaction with your current approaches. Maybe you have always taken easy courses because you want to earn A's, but you feel frustrated by your lack of intellectual growth. If you feel that earning A's is more important than growing—in other words, if your current outcomes are tolerable—the Hack won't be useful. Perhaps you doubt you can adapt and succeed in a new situation, and therefore you've remained in your existing job. Unless you are totally bored or frustrated with a lifetime of underemployment, then the Hack is unnecessary for this situation. Maybe you have been in an unsatisfying relationship for years, but is the situation depressing or annoying enough to compel you to act? Only *you* know when to consider an alternative approach, but generally, initiating change requires significant and consistent dissatisfaction: the cure has to be less painful than the disease.

To use the *Reflection Hacks* successfully, you must examine strategy decisions retrospectively, asking yourself, "What other alternatives were available?" You might use the *Stone Tablet Hack* (p. 174), which advocated writing down goals, to work through this reflection. The process of writing often makes the unconscious conscious. As you probably realize by this point in the book, automatic thinking is easy to fall into, as are habitual patterns of behavior that once worked. Habitual thinking and behavior are tied to static goals. Thus, when you modify your strategies, do so consciously and deliberately, while also reconsidering your goals and examining the contexts you find comfortable.

48. Benchmark Hack—*Think of a previously successful challenge. Apply the same methods to an unfamiliar task.*

The details
My childhood friend KB, an intelligent, witty, nerdy kind of dude, pulled off a textbook example of precision planning and operational brilliance aimed at the wrong goals. Fifteen-year-old KB dreamed of

owning a business, and his plan to get the seed money for his business involved robbing a 7-Eleven convenience store. He convinced the Fearsome Fivesome (p. 3) that his plan was foolproof. He knew where the cash was stashed, he had monitored employees' schedules and customer traffic to determine the best time to pull the job, and he was meticulously prepared for the heist: he had the right clothes, a plastic replica of a .38 Special (in case his polished communication skills failed), and a street map to ensure a quick escape. We discouraged him, but he executed his plan without a hitch and pulled off the robbery. If not for one minor detail, he would never have been arrested: KB robbed the store in which he worked.

The episode showcased KB's exceptional planning, time management, and organizational skills. If he had only applied his talent in a more productive way! Now think about the last time you excelled at something. I don't mean a typical performance when you merely accomplished your goals, but a situation that required effort, knowledge, and preparation where you hit a personal home run: crushing an athletic performance, winning a debate, acing a test, solving a persistent problem, or winning a game of chess. Which task you choose doesn't matter. (I hope you don't undercut yourself by refusing to take credit for success or downplaying your accomplishments; if you do, instead think of a friend, coworker, or relative and analyze their accomplishments.) The *Benchmark Hack* teaches us that by reflecting on a mastery experience, we can identify the process we used to succeed and apply that process to other tasks, because procedural task aspects are transferable and consistent.

Why it works

To solve a problem, you first have to clearly articulate it—a tricky task for motivational challenges. You must also suspend your beliefs, think without bias, and commit to solving the problem—dispositions that take practice and feedback. For example, let's assume you are struggling to pass a course. To identify the problem, you would scrutinize the teacher's methods, the learning materials, and your study habits. You would evaluate your existing knowledge, calculate how much you value completion, and pinpoint the motivation you need to persevere through obstacles. Any one of these factors could be the problem. People tend to focus on the desired outcome and are too impatient to carefully evaluate multiple solutions. Make one faulty inference and you will be investing effort toward the wrong area or into a strategy that isn't right for that problem (as described in the Against the *Wind Hack* [p. 209]).

Once the problem is clearly identified, the *Benchmark Hack* asks you to transfer knowledge and success from one situation to another. Businesses do this all the time—they identify and adapt industry best practices to their own business models. This Hack asks you to identify your own best practices that have helped you succeed in the past, and to adapt those strategies to current situations. KB, who chose a terrible way to solve his business capital problem, demonstrated several skills that could be leveraged for success on a different (less illegal) task. To effectively transfer knowledge, you must identify similarities between a prior successful experience and a current problem, critically examine your prior behavior, and choose the right aspects to replicate. I lost touch with KB and don't know if he transferred his astute planning, attention to detail, and organizational prowess to a career in a project management, accounting, or architecture. But I do know that, given the effort he invested in his early endeavors, applying those skills in a different context would have returned far greater rewards than stealing a measly two hundred dollars *and* getting caught.

Application
No one knows better than you how you excel. After critical evaluation, choose an existing strength and capitalize on it. Assume that everyone has transferable skills; the student who cracks jokes in class is skilled at gaining attention, the teenage girl who spends hours combing her hair and putting on makeup has a keen eye for perfection and attention to detail, and the kid who spends all day watching sports probably knows more about averages and probabilities than many mathematicians. Next, identify a moderately challenging task that will get you a desired result and generate feelings of accomplishment; picking an overly easy task won't require

enough effort to produce those feelings of accomplishment, and overly challenging tasks may mean failure and frustration.

Whichever activity you choose, be sure you understand the new challenge well enough to know what knowledge is transferable. I have enough experience in psychology to write a book, but I wouldn't be able to effectively convert the book into a podcast because I lack experience with broadcasting or recording technology. (I could learn these skills, obviously, but writing and podcasting don't require similar enough skill sets for me to apply the *Benchmark Hack* here.) Also, remember that sometimes transferring skills in which you're expert can slow down your progress on new tasks—a PhD trying to have a casual conversation with a student may not succeed because she uses too many six-syllable words. Most importantly, successful transfer requires you to know when your motivation is at its best. Ask yourself some questions. Do you need others to support you, or can you tackle something unfamiliar alone? Do you truly value attaining your chosen outcome, or will you slack off when you encounter a minor complication? Will obstacles or failure deflate you to the point of giving up? If you answered "yes" to any of these questions, reevaluate your goal before you act.

49. Under the Rug Hack—*Do not repress thoughts of perceived inadequacies.*

The details

Next let's examine a counterproductive strategy that many of us use at one time or another—glossing over reality. Recall the times when you have intentionally avoided unpleasant thoughts, or said, "I don't want to think about it." The *Under the Rug Hack* teaches us to deliberately stop avoiding reality, because repression stops growth. When you use the *Under the Rug Hack*, you intentionally attend to the people, events, contexts, or results in your life that make you uncomfortable. This Hack differs from the *Wake-Up*

Hack (p. 72), which focused on making unconscious thoughts conscious, and from the *Reality Hack* (p. 154), which focused on productive reactions to *external* events that you cannot control. The *Under the Rug Hack* is evaluative, focusing on what you can control, and reminding you that acknowledging faults and addressing challenges primes you to grow.

Repression shuts down any opportunity for development. It seems absurd to expect growth without effort, but some people expect spontaneous improvement. Repression can usually be traced to one of three causes. First, some people are simply not willing to work hard and invest the effort needed to make a change. Second, people may want to change, but not know how. Third, some people believe that their situation can't be changed and do nothing.

Why it works

We have all heard stories about children raised by wolves. These children adapt to wild environments to survive, and attempts to train them to live in human society never really succeed. They may make moderate progress, but none of the classic examples have ever completely assimilated. This is because they have no real motivation to change their existing standards and values. To grow, people must believe that change will benefit them; the first step in the change process is acknowledging dissatisfaction with an existing situation. This doesn't happen, by the way, when a helpful parent, teacher, or partner points out your faults—something that is more likely to make you defensive than motivate you to change. The conflict that provokes change is internal, a subconscious feeling that there must be a better way.

One reason we resist change is our tendency to ignore any information we see as unnecessary. This is called the *Blindness Bias*, a phrase usually used to explain why we miss things that are right in front of our faces. Without looking down, do you remember your shirt color? About 50 percent of people don't—shirt color is unimportant once you are dressed, just as some self-beliefs are unimportant once we've accepted them as part of who we are.

It works the same way with motivation: we see what we want to see because it works for us, and unless someone points out a problem, we tend not to notice our oversight unless we are intentional and deliberate in looking for it. Lucky for you, reader, you know the *Awareness Hacks* (p. 71), so you won't need to depend on other people to point out your faults and your blind spots.

There are two other reasons we shovel shit under the psychological rug, and both are neutralized by the *Under the Rug Hack*: self-justification bias and everyone's favorite self-handicapping strategy, the wooden leg. Self-justification bias means we seek to justify our behavior to ourselves in order to avoid the stress generated by believing we messed up. Sometimes this bias is useful; for example, when we commit to a decision, we are better off rationalizing the decision as a good one than spending our time ruminating over the potential wrongness of a done deal. But understanding this doesn't fix the fundamental reason you use the strategy in the first place—to avoid anxiety. The wooden leg operates under a similar principle: it uses a single catchall excuse to shift motivational energy away from a problem that should be fixed. If you often justify lack of progress by thinking or saying the same tired excuse—"I can't find a job," "My dog died," "My computer broke," or "I broke up with my boyfriend last month"—then it's not your wooden leg holding you back; it's your unwillingness to change.

Application
It's probably a good time to find your to-do list—not the one that reminds you to buy eggs, milk, and chicken wings, but the one filled with the back-burner objectives you've been meaning to start for ages. Look at the goals you put off because they are time consuming or require hard work. (There might be a lot of them!) I'm talking about things like getting a better job, making more money, finding more satisfying relationships, exercising more—anything people rarely get around to acting on. Don't worry about why the item was ignored; instead, look back at what you *did* get done and see what you overlooked. Once you've reviewed the list, pick *one* of these languishing objectives on which to refocus your efforts. Don't try

to work toward multiple objectives—when you fail, you're likely to self-justify, and that's what we're training you not to do.

Be realistic, but avoid resignation: don't slip into feeling you have accomplished enough, or that you have done everything you can under the circumstances. Accomplishing *something* doesn't mean you're finished! I often see this when students study for exams: they buckle down for an hour and then decide that they've done enough. Sure, take a fifteen-minute break and walk around or get a drink of water, but an hour probably isn't enough study to master a semester's worth of content for a final exam; academic success is measured by what has been learned and what still needs to be mastered. Seeing small accomplishments as significant is another aspect of the self-justification mentality. Making your bed after two weeks of ignoring the mess doesn't qualify as productive by most standards—doing the bare minimum doesn't deserve applause or cookies.

50. Oops Hack—*Making errors is a great way to refine motivational strategy, if you analyze why you failed.*

The details

Motivational errors occur all the time in performance-based fields like athletics and business. However, my students often provide me with excellent examples of motivational lapses and errors because they are still in the business of learning life. When I met Amy, she was eighteen and starting college. She lived on campus and was studying to become a kindergarten teacher. She was raised by con-servative and religious parents who believed self-control was a vir-tue. Amy, like most first-year college students, was thrilled to be on her own and was sowing her oats. While (unlike student Bobby) she stayed out of phone booths and didn't spend class time play-ing pinball (p. 18), she rarely missed a chance to socialize. She spent most of her first week on campus visiting sorority houses to determine which groups had the best parties. During her first two years, she changed her major twice so she could take the same classes as her best friends. By graduation, her GPA had fallen to a paltry 2.8—not very appealing to employers. She couldn't find a job, so she applied to graduate school, where her behavior patterns continued; she was dismissed after a year for not meeting program requirements. Amy eventually found a teacher's aide position. Last time we spoke, she seemed to have no regrets— she said she was happy and satisfied working in a school for ten dollars an hour.

Did Amy make mistakes in judgment or were her motivations flawed? If we examine her behavior from a value perspective (as described in the *Investment Hack* [p. 105]), it seems Amy's decisions were justified by her motives: she simply valued socializing more than grades or studying, and acted on this motivation by deciding to spend time with friends at the expense of academics. Amy was satisfied with her outcomes and now looks back fondly on her university experience. She doesn't need the *Oops Hack* because her academic strategies were not errors. They reflected her choices, and she did not wish to change her performance. The *Oops Hack* is most useful for people who meet three conditions: they are still learning the ropes, their self-beliefs are still in transition, and they want to improve. To optimize the Hack, review previous performances and identify moments when a different strategy might have produced better results. It's especially important that you recognize your errors yourself. People learn much more when they identify their own errors than when a teacher, boss, or parent points them out.

Why it works
Motivational behavior is learned, and while learning requires intelligence and ability, the best predictors of learning are relevant background knowledge and strategy choice during the learning process. Successful learning behaviors include paying attention, effectively filing and storing information in memory, attaching meaning to new information, and repeatedly using the information to avoid forgetting.

It is extremely effective to learn from past errors. Our memory is structured to recognize errors; even when we don't know the right answer, we usually know quite clearly when we are wrong. Errors stick out in our minds, making a lasting mental impression that helps us recognize the correct answer. If we are looking for the hardware department and mistakenly wind up in women's lingerie, we will never make that same mistake again, and we are more likely to get off at the right floor next time.

In other words, memory is contextually driven. If you have ever forgotten something and had to walk back into the room where you were thinking about it, you have figured out that you can jump-start the memory retrieval process by physically returning to the place that cued the memory. Neurologically speaking, the correct answer is located near the mistake, just beyond our cognitive reach. For example, if I asked you who played Jeremy Gray in the movie Wedding Crashers, you won't think about athletes—you will begin to scan your memory for actors. You may recall the face or hair color of the actor who played Gray, and you may rule out some people who didn't play the role: it wasn't Owen Wilson (he played John Beckwith in the movie). Even though you may have to look up the dark-haired guy who played the part, the error trace of Owen Wilson will remain, and thinking of Owen Wilson will always bring with it the thought, "didn't play Jeremy Gray in Wedding Crashers." Our memory of strategies works almost in the same way.

Application
From a teaching perspective, focusing on error effectively helps students remember how to avoid wrong responses and allows learners to question their methods. What motivational errors have you made? Have you chosen a bad strategy, or used a good strategy on the wrong problem? Remember the Under the Rug Hack (p. 215), and try not to let negative feelings and defensiveness keep you from thinking about these errors. And since we tend to remember events more favorably as time goes by, focus on recent events that you probably recall fairly accurately. So, what have you regretted lately?

Have you gone on a job interview and answered a different question than the one you were asked? Perhaps you criticized someone's reputation or identity instead of addressing the person's behavior? Perhaps you acted like a jerk in a subtle attempt to drive someone away? Any of these situations are prime opportunities to use the *Oops Hack* to examine your errors and figure out whether a different approach would have produced better results. When you use the *Oops Hack*, don't only focus on outcomes; examine all the circumstances of a decision and explore why you made the choice you did. You can also use the *Oops Hack* on other people—all of you perfect readers out there who never make mistakes can apply this Hack to identify motives and pinpoint poor strategy use in others' behavior. I'm being sarcastic here, but you may remember from Myth 4 (p. 57) that we all believe our own ways of thinking are better than others'. If you truly can't identify a situation where you chose the wrong strategy, try harder! Use your social comparative motives and see how the *Oops Hack* can save those less fortunate than you! Your friends and family will surely love you for it.

51. Coach Hack—*Good coaches don't point fingers or blame; they show performers how to improve.*

The details
Speaking of mistakes, I have made dozens of foolish errors—many of them are described in Chapter One (p. 2). It's sometimes hard for me to decide which of my blunders was the worst. One thing they had in common, though, was how quick other people were to blame me for my goofiness, rather than try to help me figure out what I could have done better. Typically, after a mistake (our own or other people's), we quickly pin the blame on one person. When I literally got caught with my pants down (p. 11), none of the camp counselors considered their contributory negligence—if the boys hadn't had free access to the girls' dormitory, I wouldn't have acted on my dumb, impulsive little-kid idea. But the

counselors immediately blamed my accomplice and me for our supposed carnal urges and doled out immediate, severe punishment.
Nobody talked to us or asked us any questions before humiliating
us. They certainly didn't think about how they could have prevented
the pajama incident from happening. Google "who is to blame"
and you will see over seventy million topics listed in the search
autocomplete bar, from determining who was responsible for the
"election of Donald Trump" to calculating reasons for "the soaring
cost of cauliflower."

Successful people don't worry about blame; they focus on
improving performance. When I wrote the textbook *Motivation
for Learning and Performance*, I interviewed many famous and
successful people for examples of motivated behavior. One of the
approaches frequently used by people like financier Bernard Madoff,
Emmy-winning actress Cheryl Hines, Kansas City Chiefs' Hall-of-
Fame kicker Nick Lowery, and Congressman Darren Soto was a
diligent focus on learning from mistakes. Each of these people
expected to fail sometimes; instead of feeling inadequate or defensive when they did, they chose to leverage their errors and make
changes to how they approached the next challenge. The *Coach
Hack* teaches you not to blame others, and it also reminds you not
to blame yourself. Harsh self-criticism doesn't help you grow; it par-
alyzes you. Instead, the *Coach Hack* tells you to reframe mistakes
as learning opportunities, shifting your focus off blame and onto
revising your strategies for future success.

Why it works

Not surprisingly, a thinking bias underpins our impulse to cast blame
instead of focus on post-error improvement. Myth 6 (p. 60)
explained that humans always want to understand why things
happen. In prehistoric times, gaps in causal knowledge could kill
you: knowing why things happened (why your daughters were kid-
napped or what caused plants to grow) was essential for longevity
and procreation. Millions of years later, we still look for causes, but
these days it's for psychological survival: we want to justify our
actions and feel good about ourselves. We like to see ourselves

as responsible for good outcomes, but we like to blame others for poor outcomes. If a speeding driver zooms past, do you think "Oh, that poor woman must be rushing home to care for her sick child"? Or do you think "What's wrong with that damn nincompoop?" We perpetuate the attribution bias when we justify our own behavior and criticize the behavior of others.

In addition to helping correct the attribution bias, the *Coach Hack* boosts performance by encouraging us to seek out and accept objective feedback. If we don't understand why things went wrong, we can't make corrections, so we default to blaming. The famous people I interviewed all shared a second behavior pattern: each person relied on feedback from a respected source to keep them focused, provide improvement suggestions, and guide them through motivational lapses. If it weren't for Cheryl Hines's sister Rebecca, Cheryl might have quit show business after getting rejected three times for the same part. Activist Amanda Boxtel, who spent twenty-two years in a wheelchair, might have never

YouTube video: Coach

walked unassisted again without support and guidance from friends and family who helped her accept the fact of her disability. We progress most efficiently when others support our desire to change and when they give feedback on our efforts. Just as a map helps us efficiently reach a destination without driving in haphazard circles, the coaches we choose keep us on track and moving efficiently toward our goals.

Application

Embracing the *Coach Hack* means a mental shift away from defensiveness in response to feedback; it means readjusting the belief that mistakes signify lack of ability. When using the Hack, self-blame is ignored, and feedback is viewed as a developmental opportunity that promotes changes and sustains growth. Think about how students respond to feedback from their professors. When receiving project feedback that asks for greater clarity or detail, one student might respond defensively, saying "I found your evaluation of my work to be unjustified, highly critical, and hurtful." This student blames the instructor (who is trying to help the student improve their work) and makes no revisions. Another student, who perceives the exact same feedback as enhancing learning, will use the information to make targeted revisions. Clearly, the latter student is applying the *Coach Hack*. Which student is more likely to turn in a better paper, in this class and in future classes? Clearly, the one who embraces feedback and coaching.

Use the *Coach Hack* in any situation where improving your performance might rev up your motivation to achieve. It's easy to get discouraged when things aren't going as planned; our motivation breaks down when we think we can't win, or when the effort needed to win seems too high. The *Coach Hack* can reverse feelings of inadequacy from subpar results or guilt from lack of effort; hone your focus, do an honest and complete self-evaluation, and make progress. Use the *Coach Hack* in any situation that has frustrated you, including lingering relationship issues, highly competitive work situations, or overwhelming projects. Focusing on outcomes and potential failures can make you more inclined to give up. But if failure is an opportunity to learn and improve, not a body blow to your sense of self, you will be much more likely to step into the ring and stay standing.

52. Growth Hack—*Supernatural motivation occurs only when we believe results are a function of effort, not ability.*

The details

Thomas Edison, the inventor of the light bulb, tested over six thousand different types of materials before he found a substance suitable for the economical manufacture of light-bulb filaments. The parents of the world's most famous scientist, Albert Einstein, believed he was abnormal because he did not speak until age four. Basketball legend Michael Jordan missed over nine thousand shots in his illustrious NBA career. It took J. K. Rowling six years and twelve publisher rejections before her first Harry Potter book was published. Were these people lacking in ability? Hardly. Their success and their fame came from relentless effort that gradually propelled them to greatness.

Why do some people persevere through obstacles and others easily give up? This question has inspired centuries of ramblings from philosophers like Aristotle and Charlie Sheen and me. The *Cap Hack* (p. 93) described how we limit ourselves with beliefs about potential knowledge gains. The *Growth Hack* broadens this, telling us that motivation to achieve is severely limited by the belief that success is a function of existing ability. Motivation can only reach its peak when we believe that effort, not ability, is the limiting factor of achievement. The *Growth Hack* does *not* mean that wanting something enough compensates for a lack of knowledge or skills. If you believe that disappointing outcomes are caused by lack of ability—too little experience, insufficient skill, minimal support from others, any conditions beyond your control—you are rationalizing. You are fooling yourself and constraining your own personal growth. Desired outcomes are, of course, *limited* by skill deficiency, but eliminating skill gaps is a function of effort, not ability.

Why it works
According to legendary psychologist Carol Dweck, the strongest factor driving human behavior is our belief about mindset. Dweck's lifetime of research is based on the simple notion that there are two mindsets: some people believe that even when they work hard, circumstance and personal limitations inhibit their success, and others see the world as the land of opportunity, believing that change and growth are always possible. People with a growth mindset believe that nothing is beyond their grasp and potential. The growth-mindset person is often seen as a lifelong learner—someone who is intellectually curious and is open to trying new things. People with a fixed mindset believe that success comes from inborn ability, a kind of genetic superiority. The fixed mindset views Michael Jordan as being a born athlete and discounts the decades of practice that helped Jordan become a world-class talent.

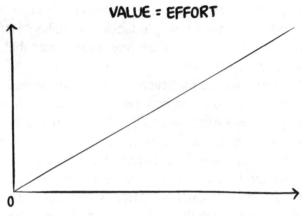

As value increases, effort rises.

Mindset beliefs are rooted in how people account for their own successes and failures. Some of us believe in effort above all, and think success is generated through passion and hard work. Others believe in ability, and think goals are achieved because of talent or sheer luck. Determining whether you are on Team Effort or Team Ability is easy. Team Effort people rarely take no for an answer. They show enthusiasm about meeting unfamiliar people, traveling to exotic places, and eating new foods, and they seek novelty and adventure. Team Effort people know that personal and professional development are achieved by focused attention, intense drive, and a willingness to learn. Team Ability people are more introspective and cautious; they prefer to undertake tasks in their areas of expertise with a high probability of success. Team Ability people covet stability, want to protect the status quo (p. 108), and see familiarity as necessary to avoiding anxiety and stress. Team Ability members are often quite successful, but their success can be limited by their fixed-mindset beliefs.

Application

Tipoffs that the *Growth Hack* might be called for include thinking or saying things like "I can't," "I don't want to," or "I'm not interested." These statements often disguise a reluctance to move forward or take on challenging, risky tasks. When people who say these things are asked "Why don't you want to?" they typically respond in a circular way: "Because that's the way I feel," "Just because," or "Whatever." These kinds of vague declarations often serve as a smoke screen—a strategy designed to direct attention away from a private source of anxiety or insecurity. People are often unwilling to think or verbalize self-doubt because they think it means they lack ability and because they fear failure. Unless these feelings of reluctance or insecurity are openly confronted, the undisclosed anxiety may render the *Growth Hack* useless for some people.

To determine when you should use the *Growth Hack*, try to understand why the person is reluctant—the cause of their stubbornness or indecision. Those who don't want to go to graduate school, can't travel abroad, or avoid meeting people often fear uncertainty and don't know if they can thrive in an unfamiliar or potentially difficult situation. Don't underestimate the extraordinary leap of faith made by a fixed-mindset person when they commit to doing something unfamiliar. It often helps to pair fixed- and growth-mindset people together. Team Effort people take pride in sharing their experiences and will feel gratified by helping other people reach their potential, creating unity and promoting mutual trust.

●

This final set of Hacks was designed to show you the factors and beliefs that can constrain personal growth and to suggest supplemental strategies to help you feel better about the inevitable failures along the way. Hindsight is 20/20; we can't look back and determine what we could have done differently until after we have tested our achievements against our target thresholds. We have to get over the disappointment of failure in order to move forward, and we have to change the strategies that didn't work. If you resist change, you're as likely to succeed as a poor sailor who listens to a hurricane forecast and goes out sailing with a broken compass and torn sails. Without appropriate preparation, neither you nor the sailor will reach your desired destination.

Warning
Now You're
Ready to
Go Hack Yourself

Prescription not required

ARGUABLY, THE MOST MOTIVATIONAL lyrics of the 1980s were authored by the punk-rock band The Clash. Go listen to the song "Should I Stay or Should I Go." Go on—I'll wait. (It's on YouTube.) The song's chorus sums up how many of us navigate the world and our daily lives. Don't let The Clash fool you! If you have read this far, you know that no outsiders, loved ones, or books can give you reasons to "stay" or "go." You are the one and only judge of what drives your unique feelings of satisfaction and joy, and you have to make up your own mind about what to do.

You may now make the "go" decision without hesitation. The Hacks you have learned are grounded in the teachings of positive psychology and aim at contributing to your long-term feelings of well-being. Think of these Hacks as cost-free prescriptions with no negative side effects, designed to get you out of bed on those tough or indecisive days. When you use the Hacks correctly, you will accomplish more with less effort, and will know what to do if things get rough. Considering the benefits described, doesn't it make sense to *Go Hack Yourself*? And then tell someone else to go get Hacked. They will thank you!

●

If you enjoyed *Hack Your Motivation*, we want to know. Please send any comments to hackyourmotivation@gmail.com. We are especially interested in reader questions.

For more information and videos of Drs. Hoffman and Feenstra discussing the Hacks, please access www.hackyourmotivation.com and our YouTube channel.

Index of Hacks

Dr. Bobby Hoffman is an Associate Professor of Educational Psychology at the University of Central Florida (UCF). Before becoming the unconventional, zany professor known for "telling it like it is," he spent twenty years working as a performance improvement consultant for some of the world's most successful global companies, including GE, NBC, KPMG, and the NBA. Dr. H. has authored more than fifty publications in psychology, management, and human resources, has been appointed to leadership positions with the world's largest educational and psychological research organizations, and serves on several journal editorial boards. When he's not busy teaching courses in motivation, learning, and cognition, he is bicycling around the globe or painstakingly trying to master the Italian language.